MENDOCINO MORNINGS

A collection of breakfast delights
from the Joshua Grindle Inn.

Mendocino Artist - Erin Dertner
(Joshua Grindle Inn, Watercolor)

Sunlight and sea, cottages and bright flowers have been North-Coast artist Erin Dertner's inspiration since the age of nine. The challenge to capture that perfect country landscape or the lush cottage garden continues to evoke the response, "Can't we live there?!"

She has won awards in national juried competitions and travels both here and abroad to gain new perspective as well as to teach. She began painting in watercolor but has added both pastels and oils to her credit and enjoys the diversity and challenge that each medium presents. Her subject matter ranges from portraits to cottages and coastal vistas, rugged landscapes and European street scenes.

Increased demand for her work over the years has led her to make them more widely available through prints, cards, calendars, and needlework kits. Her husband, Tomas, is also her business partner and oversees the marketing as well as the framing of all her work.

Erin's work is on display at Gallery One in Mendocino, a few short blocks from Joshua Grindle Inn.

Mendocino Mornings

ERIN DERTNER

By Arlene & Jim Moorehead

ACKNOWLEDGMENTS

We have many people to thank for the realization of this cookbook including, most importantly, our guests, for whom this book was created. After so many requests for recipes and suggestions to do a cookbook and on top of that, a great response to our contest for naming the title, we're finally making it happen. Of course it is all of your smiling hungry faces in the morning, in our breakfast room, that have inspired us to create and perfect these delicious recipes in the first place.

We thank our valued employees, Manager Christine Wagner and Innkeeper Sydney Weaver, who worked so diligently to make this project a success. Diane Gunnerson also made a significant contribution during the development stages. Without their efforts, this cookbook would exist only in our imaginations.

-Arlene & Jim

Library of Congress Catalog Card Number: 96-95148
Arlene & Jim Moorehead.

Book design by Fine Design Group, San Francisco.

Illustration by David Regan.

Watercolor used on cover and on page 3 by Erin Dertner.

Joshua Grindle Inn
44800 Little Lake Road
P.O. Box 647
Mendocino, CA 95460
707.937.4143
1.800.GRINDLE
www.joshgrin.com

WELCOME...

to the kitchen of the Joshua Grindle Inn! When Joshua built his home in 1879, who would have thought it would become a haven of solitude for those seeking respite from the pressures of late 20th century society? A place where one could enjoy a beautiful cozy room, good company, and best of all, a warm, deliciously prepared breakfast. We wish for you to take those memories home not only in your mind, but into your own kitchen as well. We have been serving breakfast to our Inn guests since 1989, the year we moved away from our corporate careers and city life in San Francisco. After enjoying years of successful and challenging assignments, we came to Mendocino to live a slower paced life at the Joshua Grindle Inn. We had first encountered the pleasures of the bed and breakfast experience in 1971. Our many travels since then have provided us with the knowledge and love for the travel and innkeeping business, good wine, and delicious food!

Although we both enjoy entertaining and preparing and serving food, Arlene is the true master-mind behind the breakfast menus. She has created, tested, and perfected hundreds of recipes. When guests began asking for copies to take home, we began creating a file in our computer. When guests realized we had the information in digital format, they began asking when we would compile the best ones into a published collection. Thus, we bring you, "Mendocino Mornings". Provided are many tips and serving suggestions to make the most of your creation. Whether it be for a casual breakfast on the deck or a brunch for twenty, you are sure to delight the hearts and appetites of many.

Enjoy and Bon Appetit!

Arlene and Jim Moorehead

TABLE OF CONTENTS

HISTORY OF MENDOCINO & JOSHUA GRINDLE INN

Mendocino began as a small mill town in 1852, supplying lumber from the abundant surrounding redwood forests for the upstart city of San Francisco to the south. By 1890, Mendocino had grown to 3,000 settlers from all over the world, but predominantly from northern New England. The settlers brought with them the personal imprint of their heritage which has made a lasting impression upon the quaint village.

Situated on a knoll overlooking Mendocino and the blue Pacific, the Inn reflects the New England heritage of it's original owner, Joshua Grindle, who came from Surrey, Maine to make his fortune in the booming redwood lumber business. As a raftsman for the Mendocino Lumber Company, he met and married Alice Hills, and as a wedding present from Alice's father, was given land to build his home next door to the Hills' residence. Construction on the two-story farmhouse began in 1879. Sadly, Alice died in childbirth and did not see the house completed. Joshua remarried and eventually became the town banker and primary owner of the Bank of Commerce on Main Street. The bank was later sold to A.P. Giannini and became the Bank of America. The building still stands today housing shops and offices and is known as the "Old Bank Building".

Joshua lived here until his death in 1928. Not until 1967 did the house leave the hands of the Grindle descendants. In 1978 the home became Mendocino's first small bed and breakfast inn. The Inn now has ten rooms in three buildings: the Main Grindle House, the Saltbox Cottage, and the dramatic three story Water Tower. With its two beautifully landscaped acres, Joshua Grindle Inn provides a peaceful, romantic setting for the quick weekend getaway or a midweek respite.

Nothing is more inviting than walking into a room full of smiling faces in the morning with a hot, steaming pear waiting for you at your place at the table. Fresh and baked fruits make a wonderful first course to any breakfast or brunch—preparing and cleansing the palate and oftentimes providing that early morning sugar-start so many of us need. Here we present a variety of recipes for hot fruit dishes using apples, pears, blueberries, peaches, and any other kind of fruit you have on hand or that are in season. Our award-winning pear recipe was easy to develop because we have such an abundance of healthy pear orchards just over the hill, and fresh ripe pears in our local stores daily. These hot fruit dishes accompany many of the egg and muffin recipes to follow, but we also suggest a platter of fresh fruit or a compote. The Mendocino Farmers Market is held every Friday just three blocks away from the Inn during the summer and fall months, so we always head down there and stock up on fresh, locally grown organic produce to serve with breakfast. Our favorite tradition is our Saturday morning nectarine and strawberry platter. We hope some of these recipes become a tradition with your family too!

GRINDLE HOUSE DELIGHTS & THE VILLAGE OF MENDOCINO

chapter one

FRUIT DISHES TO START OFF THE MORNING

Arlene's Spicy Baked Pears with Yogurt

Preheat oven to 350 degrees.

5 LARGE RIPE PEARS

½ CUP DARK BROWN SUGAR

¾ CUP ORANGE JUICE
   *or enough to make 1/2 inch
   of liquid in baking dish*

¼ CUP BUTTER

CINNAMON

MACE

PINCH OF GROUND CLOVES

VANILLA YOGURT

These pears are an enduring favorite and won the 1989 California Summer Fruits Bed & Breakfast Inns Recipe contest! This recipe makes a great breakfast starter, but is also a tasty dessert treat when served warm with a little vanilla ice cream or crème fraîche.

Line bottom of 10x15 inch baking dish with the brown sugar. Sprinkle sugar layer generously with cinnamon, mace and pinch of clove. Slice pears in half; remove cores and stems. Lay pears cut side down on sugar mixture. Pour orange juice over pears and dot with butter. Bake for 15-20 minutes, or until pears are tender.

To serve, place pear cut side down on a serving dish and pour some of the juice mixture over the pear. Place a dollop of yogurt along side of the pears and top with freshly grated nutmeg.

Serves 10.

Note: This recipe can be prepared in advance by combining all the ingredients except the orange juice. Pour over just before baking.

BLUEBERRY NECTARINE CRISP

Preheat oven to 350 degrees.

FILLING:

4 CUPS NECTARINES, *thinly sliced*

8 OUNCES BLUEBERRIES, *fresh or frozen*

1 TEASPOON LEMON OR ORANGE
PEEL, *grated*

1 TABLESPOON LEMON JUICE

3 TABLESPOONS SUGAR

¼ TEASPOON NUTMEG

TOPPING:

1 CUP QUICK ROLLED OATS

½ CUP WHITE FLOUR

¼ CUP BROWN SUGAR, *packed*

¼ TEASPOON CINNAMON

⅛ TEASPOON GROUND CLOVES

4 TABLESPOONS BUTTER
OR MARGARINE

In a large bowl combine the nectarines, blueberries, lemon or orange peel, lemon juice, sugar and nutmeg. Transfer the mixture to a lightly oiled 9x11 inch baking dish.

In a medium bowl combine the oats, flour, brown sugar, cinnamon and cloves. With a pastry blender or two knives worked in scissors fashion, cut in the butter or margarine until the mixture is uniformly crumbly. Sprinkle the topping over the fruit mixture.

Bake the crisp for 45 minutes until fruit is tender and top is nicely browned.

Serves 6-8.

No matter what the season, this wonderful crisp is a tasty addition to any morning meal. As with many of our fruit dishes this also makes a great evening dessert. Just add a scoop of your favorite vanilla ice cream and voilà!

MENDOCINO MASONIC TEMPLE

A frequently asked question at the breakfast table is, "What is that big white building with the carved figures on the spire?" It is the historic Masonic Temple whose construction took seven years to complete, commencing in 1866. Most of the construction and carving was done by Eric Jensen Albertson, a mason and an employee of the local lumber mill. Old records show that members donated $1,000, a loan was negotiated for $2,000, and some $860 was collected at various times to furnish the building. Mr. Albertson spent his spare time in a Big River beach shack carving the mythical figures which adorn the pedestal atop the Temple. He also carved the inside fluted columns, arches, and ceiling decorations in the upstairs meeting hall. The statuary atop the Temple, carved from a single piece of redwood, depicts the Angel of Death, the Hourglass of Transience, the Weeping Maiden, the Anointment of Her Hair, the Acacia Branch and the Sacred Urn, the Sundered Column, and the Book of Light–all of which are symbolic within the Masonic Order. The Savings Bank of Mendocino County purchased the building in 1977, and the lodge retained its kitchen and ornate meeting hall upstairs. The downstairs interior was remodeled to house the bank, using redwood extensively in the process. The brass cage teller windows in the branch office are reminiscent of an earlier and simpler age. The exterior of the building retains all of Mr. Albertson's architectural contributions without a hint of the commercial activities held within. The next time you are in the village, take a few moments to take in the beauty and historic nature of this fine old building.

LOOK OUT FOR THE FLOWERS

Flowers grow year-round in Mendocino. They thrive in our ocean-tempered climate. They like the fog and they are everywhere. If you order a salad in a restaurant, most likely it will be decorated with flowers. You will find them along the ocean, in the forest, and especially on our two landscaped areas.

The domestic rhododendron show off in April, peaking in May. A great place to see rhododendron, besides our Inn, is the Mendocino Coast Botanical Gardens—forty-seven lovely acres crisscrossed with enchanting paths which lead you down to the ocean through forest and meadows. Some of the rhododendron are twenty feet tall! You can also see wild rhododendron blooming profusely in the forests near the coast from mid-April through June. The pygmy forest of Van Damme State Park (two miles south of Mendocino) is also a great place to see wild rhododendron.

Late spring and early summer are the best times for viewing the low-growing wildflowers carpeting the meadows along the bluffs. Walking through the Headlands State Park surrounding Mendocino, you'll see Baby-blue Eyes, Chinese Houses, and Painted Cups. You might also find the patch of Calla Lilies that have "gone native", down behind the Ford House, south of Main Street.

For those of you not satisfied with just looking at flowers, the Mendocino Coast Botanical Gardens has plants for sale all year round. As well, Fuchsia-rama is a fun place to stop—good prices and a mind-boggling variety of fuchsia. There are also several good rhododendron nurseries around Fort Bragg. How many plants can you fit in your back seat? A recent guest found that his Mercedes Sedan could ride four comfortably.

Happy Trails!

MENDOCINO ART CENTER

The Mendocino Art Center is a dynamic center for the visual and performing arts in a setting renowned for its beauty and charm. Set in a garden of flowers and cypress trees on the rugged headlands of California's North Coast, the Art Center has become a well-known educational and resource center for teachers, students, professionals, and beginning artists. Mendocino is a world-renowned artists colony, bulging at the seams with local talent.

Offered is a wide variety of classes, workshops, exhibitions, theater productions, lectures, slide presentations, festivals, fairs, and entertainment to the public. It is the hub of art activities of the North Coast. During the spring, fall, and winter seasons the Center concentrates on ceramic and textile programs where the students work in studios six hours a day, five days a week to develop technical skills handling materials and equipment, with emphasis on developing individual technique and creativity as the result of mastery of technique. The weekends are devoted to two-day workshops which attract an impressive assemblage of renowned faculty, guest lecturers, and artists/craftspeople!

Summers at the Center blossom into a haven for all levels of students as an outstanding variety of week-long classes, one to two week workshops, exhibitions, slide lectures, potluck suppers, a summer fair, and celebrations proliferate. The classes and workshops offered include programs in textile, fiber arts, and ceramics. In addition, the fine arts, painting and drawing, sculpture, photography and calligraphy bring additional experts to the area to teach at this retreat by the sea.

Also, the Art Center's Nichols Gallery features regular shows and competitions, The Winona Gallery features emerging artists and The Showcase Gallery on Main Street displays established artists' work. As you plan your weekends or holidays away from the stress and clamor of the work-a-day world, a new or renewed acquaintance with the Art Center, where the imagination takes wing and creativity realizes itself, is surely worth the time as it is so necessary to the world we live in.

CIDER BRAISED APPLES

7 LARGE GRANNY SMITH APPLES,
cored and cut into 1/2 inch slices

1 ½ TEASPOON CINNAMON

½ TEASPOON ALLSPICE

½ TEASPOON NUTMEG

¼ CUP SUGAR

¼ CUP BUTTER

1 CUP APPLE OR PEAR CIDER

1 TABLESPOON CRYSTALLIZED
GINGER, *finely chopped*

GRANOLA

VANILLA YOGURT

The perfect dish for a cold winter's morning—just what you need to warm those toes! Try topping with dried cranberries and walnuts for a tasty twist.

In a large stew pot, toss apples with cinnamon, allspice, nutmeg and sugar. Cut butter into small pieces and mix in with apples.

Add the cider and bring to a boil. Reduce heat, cover and cook until tender, stirring occasionally, about 15-20 minutes. Remove from heat and stir in ginger. Spoon apples and juice into individual serving dishes and top with a sprinkle of granola and a dollop of vanilla yogurt.

Serves 7.

Note: Apples can be prepared in advance by combining all the ingredients except cider. Pour over immediately before cooking.

MOM'S POACHED FRUIT

Our thanks to Margaret Fox, owner of Cafe Beaujolais for sharing this great recipe of her mom's with us.

5 CUPS PREMIUM GRAPE JUICE
*such as Husch Zinfandel juice
or dry white wine, see note below*

1 CUP WHITE SUGAR

5 CINNAMON STICKS
about 3 inches long

20 WHOLE CLOVES

20 CARDAMOM SEEDS
remove seeds from the whitish pods

15 WHOLE ALLSPICE BERRIES

1 TEASPOON ANISE SEED

½ CUP LEMON JUICE, *fresh squeezed*

FRUIT: TRY PEARS, PLUMS, APPLES,
ORANGES, APRICOTS OR
OTHER FRUITS THAT ARE
FIRM ENOUGH TO HOLD UP
TO POACHING.

Place all ingredients in a large pot and simmer, uncovered, for about 5 minutes. Slice the fruit any way you wish. Add fruit, bring to a boil, cover and turn the heat down. Simmer for about 3 to 5 minutes, or until fruit is tender. Cooking time depends on the size of the fruit slices and ripeness of the fruit, so check the fruit with a sharp knife for tenderness. (You may also add the fruit in stages so that the smaller and more ripe pieces do not overcook.)

When done, remove from heat and cool. Refrigerate for at least 8 hours before serving. Serve with a spoonful of yogurt, sour cream or creme fraîche.

Serves 20.

This is great in the winter when most fruit taste like cottonballs. Use whatever is available—just remember cooking times will vary.

Note: Dry white wine can also be used, but increase the sugar; the premium grape juice is very sweet and does not require much added sugar.

HONEY BAKED APPLES

Preheat oven to 325 degrees.

5 LARGE GRANNY SMITH APPLES
HONEY
½ CUP RAISINS
½ CUP WALNUTS, *chopped*
ORANGE ZEST
APPLE OR PEAR JUICE
2 TABLESPOONS BUTTER
CINNAMON
CLOVES

Any apple will do to create this heart-warming dish for a special house guest or your loving family. All will enjoy the soothing flavors and lingering aromas.

"Excellent breakfasts & delightful company around the table–a good way to learn about the area!"
-L & J,
Pollock Pines, CA

Line the bottom of a 10x15 inch baking dish with a thin layer of honey. Halve and core apples. Set apples cut side down on honey. Sprinkle raisins, nuts, orange zest, cinnamon and cloves around apples. Cut butter into pieces and sprinkle over apples. Puncture each apple in discreet place with toothpick to allow steam to escape and prevent apples from splitting.

Pour cider over apples to 1/3 way up the side of baking dish. Bake for 30 minutes until apples are tender but still holding their shape. Serve each apple half (cut side up) in an individual dish, with a large spoonful of raisin and nut mixture in the center, and cooked juices poured over top.

Serves 10.

Variation: MAPLE ALMOND BAKED APPLES
Replace honey with maple syrup and walnuts with sliced almonds.

Note: If preparing to cook the next day, simply add juice immediately before cooking.

HOT FRUIT AND NUT COMPOTE

4 MEDIUM GOLDEN DELICIOUS
   APPLES
⅔ CUP SUGAR
⅔ CUP DRIED CRANBERRIES
⅓ CUP GOLDEN RAISINS
⅓ CUP DRIED CURRANTS
2 CUPS CRANBERRY JUICE
5 TEASPOONS ARROWROOT POWDER
½ CUP WALNUTS, *chopped*
½ CUP PECANS, *chopped*
1 ¼ TABLESPOONS LEMON JUICE

Cut apples into thin wedges and place in large saucepan. Add sugar, dried fruit, and cranberry juice to apples and combine. Bring to a boil. Lower heat and simmer for 1-3 minutes, until apples are tender. Remove from heat.

In a small bowl stir together arrowroot powder with a little cranberry juice or water. Stir into compote and return to moderate heat, stirring gently, until liquid is thickened and clear (but do not let boil). Remove from heat and cool completely. Cover and refrigerate overnight.

In the morning, add nuts and stir compote over medium heat until hot. Add lemon juice and continue stirring and cooking until apples are thoroughly tender and juice clings to compote as a glaze.

Serve in individual dishes with yogurt garnish. Makes 5 cups.

This recipe is a nice treat served with a dollop of yogurt on the side, but it also makes a wonderful topping for a vanilla ice cream sundae!

Jim's Marinated Fruit Salad

6-8 CUPS SLICED FRUIT, YOUR CHOICE:
   APPLES, ORANGES, STRAWBERRIES,
   GRAPES, PINEAPPLE, MELON, ETC.

¼ CUP BOILING WATER
¼ CUP SUGAR IN THE RAW
½ CUP ORANGE JUICE
¼ TEASPOON ALMOND EXTRACT
1 TABLESPOON POPPY SEEDS

VANILLA YOGURT

This is great for fruit that has not quite received the intensity of summer heat and needs a bit of sweetness to bring out all the flavors.

Put fruit in a large bowl. In a smaller bowl, pour boiling water over sugar and stir until dissolved. Add orange juice, almond extract, and poppy seeds to sugar and water mixture and pour over sliced fruit. Stir until evenly coated and let stand for 30 minutes. Stir again and serve with vanilla yogurt as a garnish.

Serves 8-10.

PEACH OR PEAR COBBLER

Preheat oven to 350 degrees.

FILLING:
6 PEACHES OR PEARS
¼ CUP BROWN SUGAR
½ TEASPOON CINNAMON
½ TEASPOON GINGER
¼ TEASPOON VANILLA
LEMON JUICE

TOPPING:
½ CUP BAKING MIX
½ CUP GRANOLA
2 TABLESPOONS BUTTER

Slice peaches or pears into a bowl. Sprinkle with sugar, spices, and juice. Stir until fruit is coated. Let stand for at least one hour. Pour into lightly greased 9x11 inch baking dish.

Cut butter in biscuit mix using a pastry blender until well blended. Add granola. Spread over peach mixture and dot with butter.

Bake for 30 minutes until nicely browned and crispy on top.

Serves 10.

Note: The fruit can stand overnight in the refrigerator to help meld the flavors together. Add topping immediately before cooking the next day.

"A candle's light and chilled champagne,
The sweetest smile and tears from pain.
All these were found at Grindle's Inn,
And we may come back here again."
-T & L

Remember when all there was to choose from was Quiche Lorraine and Quiche Florentine? Remember when "real men didn't eat quiche?" Well, those days are long past and we here at the Joshua Grindle Inn have embraced the Age of the Quiche (and the frittata, and the omelette, and the vegetable pie, and the baked french toast...) The greatest thing about quiches, besides being easy to prepare, wonderful tasting, and a nice presentation, is that they can be created out of almost any combination of vegetables-thus the solution to the 1/2 head of broccoli and two random tomatoes that have been sitting in the corner of your refrigerator drawer waiting to be included in a recipe. The quiche is also a very versatile dish—it is simple to make it light or substantial, and it makes a great meal any time of day! (To lighten up any of these quiches, choose low or non-fat milk, no-fat sour cream, low fat cheeses or increase the amount of veggies while foregoing the butter or oil!) We have enjoyed experimenting with alternatives to the standard flour pie crust, too. We have found that a polenta crust soaks up the flavors of the body of the quiche very nicely; a shredded potato crust makes a nice, light nest around the custard and the mushroom crust puffs up into a beautiful and unique presentation! We do love our quiches but they by no means overshadow the lovely frittatas, tasty potato dishes, and rich baked french toast we also enjoy serving. And by the way, every morning plenty of "real men" sit around our breakfast table savoring every delectable bite of quiche!

SALTBOX COTTAGE BREAKFAST DISHES & FUN
THINGS TO DO IN & AROUND MENDOCINO

chapter two

QUICHES, FRITTATAS, OMELETS & MORE

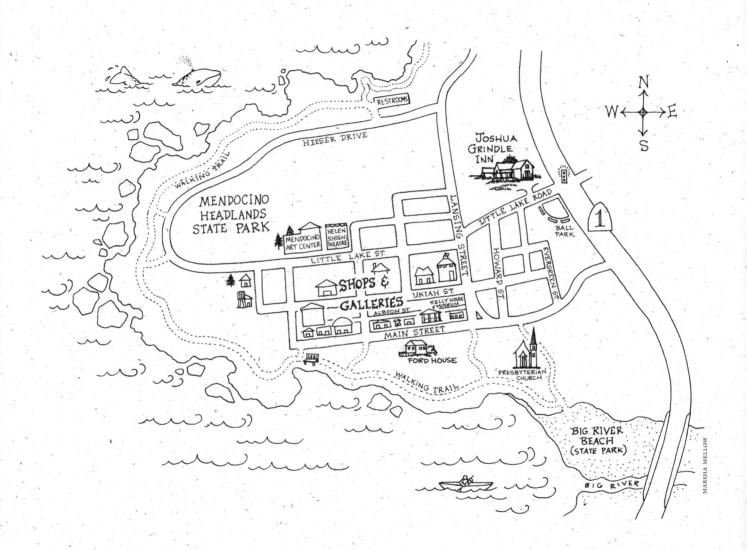

CANOEING, KAYAKING & BICYCLING

Canoeing along the scenic Big River is a delight for naturalists, photographers, and romantics. It appeals to both the novice and enthusiast alike. Paddle upstream and leave the summer coastal fog behind; enter the upper estuary where the sun is bright, the air is warm, and the river is narrow and intimate. The Big River is the longest unspoiled estuary in Northern California. Its shores remain undeveloped–there is no harbor at its mouth nor homes on its shores. This tidal stream winds it way serenely through a canyon bordered by stately firs and towering redwoods. Protected from speeding boats and jet skis, Big River is a rare sanctuary. Its salt marshes, canyons and stream beds are the homes of wood ducks, osprey, harbor seals, and a variety of other wildlife. Along its banks are century-old train trestles, wooden pilings and log dams–historic remnants of early logging. The river is brackish from the bridge to about 8 miles inland, so it is best to consult a tide table and attempt to paddle up river with the flood tide, making your return trip as the tide goes back out. The river is smooth and deep, with marshes where swallows collect mud for their nests and Great Blue Heron hunt for their meals. There is little current except for the influence of the tides and light breezes, thus it is an easy trip for those new to canoeing and kayaking–there are no rapids and waterfalls to contend with!

Whether on a mountain or road bike, bicycling is a wonderful experience in itself and offers a unique way to explore the Mendocino Coast. If your preference is a road bike, Van Damme, Russian Gulch and MacKerricher State parks offer paved trails where you can ride through the redwood and fern canyons and along the coastal streams and ocean. Little Lake Road (our street), Point Cabrillo Drive, Comptche-Ukiah Road and other paved back roads are less traveled and provide challenging rides. If your preference is a mountain bike, the Mendocino Coast is a paradise. Explore unpaved back roads, logging roads and trails, ride through redwood forests and bicycle to swimming holes along our coastal rivers. Our innkeepers are avid bike riders and can let you in on their favorite biking trails. As well, local writer Bob Lorentzen's Mendocino Coast Bike Rides provides a comprehensive guide to coast bicycling and is on sale in our gift shop. Whether on a road or a mountain bike, watch grey whales from Mendocino's headlands and bike through the back lanes of our historic village. Discover the incredible beauty of a Mendocino spring day, the quiet of a foggy summer morning, the warmth of an autumn evening, and the vivid colors of winter.

BERRY STUFFED FRENCH TOAST–SAN FRANCISCO STYLE

Prepare at least eight hours before serving.

12 SLICES SAN FRANCISCO
   SOURDOUGH BREAD
8 OUNCES LOW FAT CREAM CHEESE
1 CUP BERRIES, *your choice: fresh or frozen*

10 EGGS
⅓ CUP MAPLE SYRUP
2 CUPS LOW FAT MILK

BERRY SAUCE:
1 CUP WATER
1 CUP SUGAR
2 TABLESPOONS CORN STARCH
1 CUP BERRIES, *fresh or frozen*
1 TABLESPOON BUTTER

Is this french toast or a bread pudding? This dish is so rich, yet light, we think it may even be an improvement on bread pudding. Note that like a bread pudding, the longer it is allowed to soak before baking, the fuller the flavor.

Remove the crusts from the bread and cut into cubes. Oil a 9x13 baking dish. Spread half of the bread cubes over the bottom of the pan. Cut cream cheese into cubes and distribute over bread layer. Spread berries over the cream cheese. Place remaining bread cubes over top.

Beat the eggs, maple syrup and milk together well. Pour over bread. Cover with foil and refrigerate overnight. Press down on foil to make sure all bread is soaked.

In the morning, preheat oven to 350 degrees. Bake with foil on for 30 minutes, then remove foil and bake for an additional 30 minutes until center is set and top is lightly browned. Let stand 10 minutes before slicing. Serve with Berry Sauce.

Berry Sauce:
Stir water, sugar, cornstarch, and berries over medium heat until thickened. Add butter and stir until melted. Pour over individual pieces of french toast with a twist of lemon for decoration.

Serves 9-12.

Black Olive & Artichoke Frittata

12 EGGS

1 PINT SMALL CURD COTTAGE CHEESE

1 ½ TEASPOONS PESTO SAUCE

½ CUP FLOUR

2 TEASPOONS BAKING POWDER

½ TEASPOON SALT

¼ POUND CHEDDAR CHEESE, *grated*

¼ POUND PEPPER JACK CHEESE, *grated*

14 OUNCES ARTICHOKE HEARTS
  packed in water, drained & sliced 1/4 inch thick

2 ½ OUNCES CHOPPED BLACK OLIVES

4 GREEN ONIONS, *thinly sliced*

1 SMALL RED PEPPER, *thinly sliced*

SOUR CREAM

SALSA

Wisk eggs in cuisinart until well blended. Add cottage cheese, pesto sauce, flour, baking powder and salt, whisk again until well blended. Pour mixture into a large bowl, and add remaining ingredients except for red pepper. Pour into an oiled 9x12 oblong pan and top with red pepper slices. Bake at 350 degrees for 30-40 minutes or until eggs are just set. Cut into squares and garnish each with sour cream and salsa.

Serves 12.

"Mendocino has all the old-fashioned virtues we remember, but rarely find now in Europe. It has a wonderful peaceful feeling and everywhere there are flowers, banks of color, both cultivated and wild."

-D & L

Christine's California Frittata

Preheat oven to 350 degrees.

FOR 10 RAMEKINS:

CRUST:

1 ½ CUPS BAKING MIX

4 EGGS

¾ CUP GREEN ONIONS, *chopped & sauteed*

½ CUP MILK

FILLING:

8 OUNCES CREAM CHEESE

4 EGGS

1 CUP MUSHROOMS, *sliced*

1 CUP GREEN ONIONS, *chopped*

2 TEASPOONS GARLIC, *minced*

½ CUP SUN DRIED TOMATOES, *diced*

1 CUP BROCCOLI FLOWERS, *chopped*

2 CUPS COTTAGE CHEESE

2 CUPS PEPPER JACK CHEESE

1 10-OUNCE PACKAGE FROZEN CHOPPED
   SPINACH, *thawed and drained*

GRATED PARMESAN CHEESE

This dish can be made in a casserole or pie pan, but we really like it served in individual ramekins because they puff up beautifully and make a nice presentation. These are also great for lunch or dinner. Simply make up a batch ahead of time and store in your freezer. When ready for them just thaw and cook!

Oil 10 individual ramekins. Mix together baking mix, eggs, green onions, and milk until smooth. Divide batter evenly between ramekins. Dot with nickel-sized drops of cream cheese.

Sauté mushrooms, green onions, garlic, and sun dried tomatoes in a little oil until tender. Add broccoli and spinach and saute until evenly cooked.

In a large bowl, beat eggs thoroughly. Add cheeses and vegetable mix and stir. Distribute evenly among ramekins and top with grated Parmesan cheese.

Bake on baking sheet for 50-60 minutes, until top is puffed and brown, and toothpick comes out clean.

Serves 10.

MUSHROOM CRUST QUICHE

Preheat oven to 350 degrees.

3 TABLESPOONS BUTTER
½ POUND MUSHROOMS, *chopped*
½ CUP SALTINE CRACKERS, *crushed*
½ CUP GREEN ONIONS, *chopped*

1 ½ CUPS PEPPER JACK CHEESE, *shredded*
1 ½ CUPS SMALL CURD COTTAGE CHEESE
5 EGGS
¼ TEASPOON CAYENNE PEPPER
¼ TEASPOON PAPRIKA

In a frying pan over medium heat, melt butter. Add mushrooms and green onions and saute until tender. Stir in cracker crumbs. Turn mixture into an oiled 8-inch pie pan. Spread mixture evenly over bottom and sides of pan using a spatula, creating a 1/4 inch raised crust around edges of pie pan.

Sprinkle evenly with shredded cheese. In a food processor, whirl cottage cheese, eggs, and cayenne pepper until smooth. Pour into crust and sprinkle with paprika.

Bake for 45-50 minutes or until knife inserted in center comes out clean. Let stand 10 minutes before cutting.

Serves 10-12.

"The innkeepers were a delight and [the] Mushroom Crust Quiche is the best in the world!"
　　　　-M & E and one on the way.

MENDOCINO HEADLANDS

You haven't seen Mendocino until you've taken a walk along the Headlands. Popular for whale watching, walking, jogging, and viewing the tidepools and wildflowers. At the Southernmost tip of the trail, the headlands jut out into the sea, creating an underwater cave and blowholes which can be viewed from above. It is an awe-inspiring experience to stand over the land covering the blowholes as they moan and shake the ground beneath your feet.

The Mendocino Headlands weren't always accessible for public use and enjoyment. The land south of Main Street was once a lumber mill, with several other buildings, shops and homes along side it. With the closing of the Union Lumber Company and a great fire, most of the buildings were destroyed. In 1968, Boise Cascade announced plans to buy the Company and all its historic land holdings. There were strong rumors of a condominium project just south of Main Street. The general reaction in town was unfavorable, and local artist and activist Emmy Lou Packard decided to do something to preserve the precious coastline. Emmy Lou's appeals went far and wide, eventually receiving national publicity. C. Malcolm Watkins, Chairman of the Department of Civil History for the Smithsonian Institution, wrote in December 1968, "I do not think it is an overstatement that it appears just as important for California to have Mendocino preserved and guarded against encroachments as it was for Virginia to have Williamsburg restored and protected." The story made headlines in the Bay Area newspapers in January 1969.

Mildred Benioff met Emmy Lou at the post office in late 1968, and Emmy Lou admitted that she was great at getting projects started, but just didn't have the time to carry them through. She asked Mildred if she would take over. Mildred accepted and was soon serving as head of the Mendocino Headlands Park Committee, appointed by the State Parks Director. Mildred wrote to her friend Rudd Brown, then head of the State Department of Recreation, who first suggested the idea of a land swap, since the State had no money to buy park land. The committee began a long series of negotiations with Boise Cascade and the State Parks Department. A long struggle next ensued which included the birth of the Mendocino Historical Preservation District and Historical Review Board, a committee dedicated to preserving the special character of the Mendocino Village. The land swap finally went through in February 1972, and the Mendocino Headlands State Park was established. Emmy Lou Packard, now living in the San Francisco Bay Area, is honored by a bronze plaque (mounted on a large redwood log near the gate at the west end of Main Street) which credits her vision and perseverance towards the creation of the Headlands State Park.

FARMER'S MARKET PIE

Preheat oven to 350 degrees.

½ CUP POLENTA
1 ½ CUPS WATER
¼ CUP PARMESAN CHEESE
½ TEASPOON SALT

¾ CUP ZUCCHINI, *sliced thinly*
1 CUP MUSHROOMS, *sliced thinly*
½ CUP GREEN ONIONS, *diced*
¼ CUP SUN-DRIED TOMATOES, *chopped*
SALT AND PEPPER TO TASTE

3 EGGS, *beaten*
½ CUP COTTAGE CHEESE
¾ CUP PEPPER JACK CHEESE, *grated*
1 CUP MILK

We are lucky to have the Farmer's Market held just three blocks away from the Inn. The vegetables listed below are suggested, but any mixture of fresh vegetables can be substituted depending upon availability and, for us, whatever looks tastiest at the Farmer's Market!

Oil a large pie plate. To make polenta crust, combine water, and salt. Bring to a boil and add polenta. Stir over medium heat until thickened. Stir in Parmesan cheese and pour into bottom of pan.

Sauté zucchini, mushrooms, green onions, and tomatoes until tender. In a medium bowl, mix together eggs, cottage cheese, jack cheese, and milk. Add vegetable mixture. Pour evenly over crust.

Bake for 40-50 minutes until lightly browned on top and center is set.

Serves 10-12.

GRINDLE GARDEN QUICHE

Preheat oven to 350 degrees.

12 OUNCES FRESH OR FROZEN POTATOES, *shredded*
SALT AND PEPPER TO TASTE

1 CUP ONION, *sliced*
¼ CUP SUN-DRIED TOMATOES
½ CUP BROCCOLI, *finely chopped*
1 CUP MUSHROOMS, *thinly sliced*
2 TABLESPOONS BUTTER

2 CUPS MILK
¼ POUND FETA CHEESE, *crumbled*
¼ POUND MOZZARELLA, *grated*
4 EGGS
1 TEASPOON SALT
¼ TEASPOON PEPPER
1 TEASPOON WORCESTERSHIRE SAUCE
2-3 TABLESPOONS FRESH OR DRIED HERBS
basil, rosemary, sage, thyme, parsley, etc., finely chopped

If you've got an herb garden, by all means this is the quiche for you! This dish really highlights the vibrant flavors of freshly picked herbs. Our herb garden has several varieties of sage and rosemary which we use liberally for this creation.

Oil a large pie plate and spread potatoes evenly over bottom. Sprinkle with salt and pepper. Bake for 20-25 minutes, stirring occasionally, until slightly browned. Remove from oven and shape over bottom and sides of pan.

Sauté onions, tomatoes, broccoli, and mushrooms in butter until tender. Drain liquid and spread vegetables over potatoes. In a medium sauce pan, heat milk until almost scalding. Add feta and mozzarella and stir until melted and creamy. In a separate bowl, beat eggs with a whisk until frothy. Stir in salt, pepper, Worcestershire sauce and herbs. Add to milk mixture and stir until completely blended. Pour over vegetables.

Bake for 45-55 minutes until set.

Serves 10-12.

Joshua's Oven Baked Omelet

Prepare at least eight hours before baking.

½ LOAF SOURDOUGH BREAD, *sliced*

4 OUNCES LIGHT CREAM CHEESE

1 CUP CHEDDAR CHEESE, *grated*

1 CUP JACK CHEESE, *grated*

1 CUP GREEN ONIONS, *chopped*

¼ CUP MARINATED RED
    BELL PEPPER, *diced*

5 EGGS, *well beaten*

1 CUP MILK

¼ TEASPOON DRY MUSTARD

⅛ TEASPOON PEPPER

¼ TEASPOON CAYENNE PEPPER

This is one of the most deceptively easy recipes you'll find in this book. It is so delicious—especially the way the cream cheese melts into the bread creating a wonderful custard-like texture that it is hard to believe it takes so little time and work to prepare!

Slice crusts off of bread and cut into one inch cubes. Oil a 9x13 inch pan and place bread cubes in bottom. Dot with cream cheese. Layer cheddar, jack, green onions over bread and top with red peppers. Mix together eggs, milk, salt, mustard, and two peppers. Pour over bread. Cover with foil and press down to help bread soak up egg mixture. Refrigerate overnight.

The next day, preheat oven to 375 degrees. Bake covered on top shelf for 20 minutes, then remove foil and bake for 20 more minutes until nicely browned and bubbly on top. Let stand 10 minutes before cutting.

Serves 10.

Some variations:
- Substitute Pepper Jack for some or all of the cheese.
- Sprinkle Parmesan over the top for a final layer.
- Replace green onions and peppers with sauteed mushrooms, green onion and Roma tomato mixture.
- Top with mozzarella.

Note: The omelet can be made up to a week in advance by freezing the assembled dish before adding egg mixture. The day before, remove omelet from freezer. When thawed completely, add egg mixture and follow remaining directions.

KITCHEN GARDEN BREAD

Prepare at least eight hours before baking.

ONE ROUND LOAF SOURDOUGH
   BREAD, *bake and serve*
½ POUND MUSHROOMS, *sliced very thin*
2 MEDIUM YELLOW ONIONS,
   sliced very thin
8 OUNCES CREAM CHEESE
½ POUND HOT PEPPER JACK CHEESE,
   grated
½ CUP CHEDDAR, *grated*
1 TABLESPOON BROWN SUGAR
1 ½ CUPS FRESH HERBS AND
   VEGETABLES
   green onions, tiny broccoli flowers, chives,
   parsley, cauliflower, bell peppers, etc.
6 EGGS, *beaten*
1 CUP MILK

Grease one cookie sheet. Slice the bread in half so that you have two rounds and scoop out most of the soft center. Place on cookie sheet.

Sauté the onions and mushrooms until tender, adding the brown sugar and a little salt about half way through. Set aside. Sauté herbs and vegetable mix. Set aside.

Cut cream cheese into 1-inch cubes and distribute evenly over both bread halves and top with the onion/mushroom mixture. Sprinkle cheddar cheese over onion/mushroom mixture. Layer 1/2 of the herb/vegetable mix over the top, sprinkle on pepper jack cheese, then top with remaining herb/vegetable mix.

Mix eggs and milk together with any extra herbs you like and pour evenly over bread. Cover and refrigerate overnight if possible, or for at least eight hours.

The next day, bake at 375 degrees for 35-45 minutes until nicely browned on top and center is set. Slice into wedges with a pizza cutter or large knife. Serve hot.

Serves 16-20.

"To Us: Our hearts are happy.
Our spirits are lifted. Our souls are
mated. Our room is gifted."
            -N & J

WHALE WATCHING

Mendocino is a fabulous whale watching village. As the California Gray Whales travel south in the late fall and north in the spring with their new calves, you can view their spouts or watch them frolicking along the shoreline.

Each year from November through April, our coast is graced with the presence of these magnificent creatures as they journey from the Bering and Chukchi Seas between Alaska and Siberia to Baja California, a 10,000 mile round trip! They spend winter in the warm lagoons of Baja, have their calves, and then head back in the spring to the food-rich waters of Alaska, where they feast primarily on bottom-dwelling creatures called amphipods, and sometimes on schooling fish or swarming crustaceans. By the end of summer, each whale has gained six to twelve inches of oily blubber which will be an energy reserve during the winter months ahead.

The village of Mendocino is a prime West Coast whale-watching location with its peninsula thrusting a mile westward into the Pacific. Walking down Main Street you can see the whales spout as they go by off shore. On many of our windless, crystal clear winter days, we have sat on the front porch of the Inn and seen the spouts appear for a few seconds and disperse like fountains of mist. For a closer view, the Mendocino Headlands State Park, which surrounds the entire perimeter of the peninsula, is the place to go with your binoculars. The level trails on the rocky bluffs provide some of the best viewing spots on the Coast. Although we have seen whales come in as close as the farthest rocks, perhaps a distance of 50 yards from our vantage point, they usually will be 1/4 to 1/2 mile off shore, so binoculars will help you get a good view of their backs and flukes as they come up to breathe. For an even closer view, a charter boat is available in Noyo Harbor. We are lucky to have the chance to view these gentle giants so closely, and to watch the resurgence of a once very endangered species, first hand!

MUSEUMS

On your next visit to Mendocino, we recommend visiting the Kelley House Museum and the Ford House (Mendocino Visitors Center). They will give you a glimpse of what Mendocino was like in the late 1800's.

The Kelley House, an historic landmark, is an interesting building structurally and historically. The house was built in 1861 by William H. Kelley and is an example of "balloon construction", meaning that the vertical studs in the walls run from the main floor to the rafters. A timber beam called a ledger is connected to the studs to support the joists for the upstairs floors. The museum displays an outstanding collection of 1800's photographs of the historic houses and buildings in Mendocino, as well as family portraits and photos. The docents at the museum offer a wonderful tour of the house's five rooms as well as the gardens and pond.

The Ford House has wonderful exhibits of the lumber industry that gave Mendocino its origin. The displays include various ships and equipment used, as well as a scale model of Mendocino as it looked in 1890. The Ford House itself is an excellent example of early Mendocino architecture, as it was one of the first homes built here. It remains decorated in the style of the late 1800's, the Ford family's years here. A docent volunteer will be happy to answer any questions about the house and family. The Ford House also offers tours of town, the headlands, wildflowers, and bird walks.

MacKerricher State Park

If you're looking for a long stretch of beach, tidepools or those picturesque seals, this is the place! MacKerricher State Park, located just three miles north of Fort Bragg, offers a pleasant contrast to the hot summers experienced in many parts of California. Here, summer days are cool and sometimes foggy, and spring and fall offer spectacular clear vistas of ocean and shoreline. Winter temperatures seldom fall below freezing, and the park is a great place to watch winter storms brew and waves crash against the beach. This area, originally known as El Rancho de la Laguna, was purchased by Duncan MacKerricher in 1868. It was operated by his family until 1949, when it was gift-deeded to the State for use as a park.

The mild climate encourages the luxuriant growth of plants and trees found in the park. Though the headlands are nearly bare of trees, they are covered with a thick mat of grass and windflowers including sea pinks, wild onion, paint brush, lupine, California Poppy, and monkey flower. Further back from the ocean is a forest of Bishop and shore pine, tanoak, lowland fir, and Douglas fir. Beneath the trees are wax myrtle, cascara, salal, twinberry, and California blackberry.

In addition to being a great spot for shell collecting, the shoreline at MacKerricher is dotted with tidepools—home of small specimens of marine life such as anemone, sea urchin, starfish, an occasional octopus or giant sea chiton. . . the list is almost endless. MacKerricher is not on a main flyway, but many species of shore birds and waterfowl visit Cleone Lake during the fall and winter. Permanent residents include quail, swallows, blackbirds and jays. More than ninety species of birds have been identified. Cleone Lake has a boat ramp for human-powered crafts only and is a great spot for permit trout fishing. Perhaps the most entertaining species of wildlife to be viewed at the park are the seals, who lounge on a ridge of rock surrounded by tidepools at the end of a long boardwalk leading out to the sea from the parking lot. There is a railed platform with benches which provides a comfortable viewing area to watch the cantankerous seals, who bark and argue amongst themselves as they each try to find the sunniest spots on the rocks! There are informational diagrams about the seals displayed on the viewing deck, as well as whale information, as this is also a prime whale watching spot! Whether it be for wildlife viewing, walking, bike riding, fishing or surfing, MacKerricher State Park is a great place to spend the day!

THE SKUNK TRAIN

The California Western Railroad offers scenic train rides on their famous "Skunk" trains. The California Redwoods provide an awe-inspiring backdrop for this piece of American history. To some it seems like only yesterday when steam passenger service began and the little self-powered gas engines of 1925 prompted people to say, "you can smell 'em before you can see 'em." The Skunk line operates different trains to power your journey into the redwoods. Depending upon your travel plans, you can ride the rails on an exciting variety of equipment. The vintage 1925 MS-100 motorcar, the only remaining train of its kind in use today, as well as the 1935 MS-300 motorcar run the line all year round, while the diesel powered engine No. 64, or the famous "Ole' No. 45" Baldwin Steam Engine operate mostly during the summer months.

Forty miles of Skunk line run from the coastal town of Fort Bragg (just 15 minutes north of Mendocino on Highway One) to the inland city of Willits. For well over one hundred years, rail cars have traveled the beautiful scenic "Redwood Route" on the Skunk line carrying logs, loggers, freight and passengers through the towering redwoods and mountain meadows from the sea to warm, sunny Willits and back again. Leaving Fort Bragg, you will travel from majestic Pacific coast-line back into a landscape familiar to those who lived on the Coast a hundred years ago. The slow moving Puddin' Creek eases you along the Noyo river which leads you into the glory of the majestic and awe-inspiring redwood sequoias. A mountain tunnel and an hour later, the midway point of Northspur appears in the midst of sunny redwoods where you may disembark and enjoy a light snack at the refreshment stand before returning to Fort Bragg or continuing on to Willits. Open observation cars are available during the summer season and on many fall and spring runs, for capturing glorious photographs of the train and trestles, rivers and redwoods.

The trains begin their runs in Fort Bragg and there are one-way or round-trips from Fort Bragg to Willits. You can also escape for the morning or afternoon on one of their 3-hour excursions from Fort Bragg to the midway point of Northspur and back again. This scenic and relaxing train ride can be either a half or whole-day adventure.

DECADENT FRENCH TOAST

Prepare at least eight hours in advance.

2 TABLESPOONS CORN SYRUP

1 CUP BROWN SUGAR, *packed*

5 TABLESPOONS BUTTER OR
  MARGARINE

16 SLICES SOURDOUGH BREAD,
  crusts removed

5 EGGS

1 ½ CUPS MILK

1 TEASPOON ALMOND EXTRACT

½ TEASPOON NUTMEG

½ TEASPOON CINNAMON

SOUR CREAM

FRESH FRUIT

*"The Joshua Grindle Inn, a perfect setting
to enjoy the surrounding beauty of the
land. An added bonus, no phones, no TV,
and no radio (heaven)! We are already
planning the dates for our next visit."*
                              -G & G
                         Pleasanton, CA

Melt butter in a small, heavy saucepan. Add corn syrup and brown sugar and stir constantly until bubbly. Pour syrup into an oiled 9x11 inch pan. Nestle bread slices into the syrup making two layers. Mix together eggs, milk, almond extract and spices. Pour over bread, cover and refrigerate overnight.

The next morning place in preheated 350 degree oven and bake uncovered for 40-50 minutes or until slightly golden on top. Do not overbake, otherwise sugars will burn.

Serve immediately to prevent syrup from hardening. When serving, place pieces upside-down on plate, and serve with sour cream and fresh fruit garnish.

Serves 8.

POTATO ASPARAGUS QUICHE

Preheat oven to 350 degrees.

FOR ONE 9-INCH POTATO CRUST:

14 OUNCES FROZEN SHREDDED
  POTATOES
SALT & PEPPER TO TASTE

FOR THE CUSTARD:

1 ¾ CUPS LOW FAT MILK
5 EGGS, *beaten*
1 TEASPOON NUTMEG
SALT & PEPPER TO TASTE

FOR THE FILLING:

⅓ POUND MUSHROOMS, *sliced*
½ CUP GREEN ONIONS, *chopped*
½ CUP ASPARAGUS, *chopped*
  (save tips for garnish)
¼ POUND MONTEREY JACK CHEESE,
  grated

Oil one 9-inch glass pie plate. Distribute potatoes over bottom of pie plate and toss with salt & pepper. Bake for 20-25 minutes, until slightly browned. Remove from oven and spread potatoes evenly over bottom and sides of pan.

Place cheese on bottom of crust. Sauté mushrooms and onions and distribute over cheese. Place chopped asparagus over mushrooms and onions. Finally, combine the custard ingredients and pour into the shell. Arrange reserved asparagus tips on top in a decorative manner.

Bake for about 45-60 minutes or until custard is set and the top is puffed and brown. Serve hot, warm or at room temperature.

Serves 10.

"...as we speak, the memories of sitting in an Adirondack chair at the edge of your lawn surrounded by mounds of Spring flowers have been the catalyst for the creation of my own Olde English Garden in the front yard of my recently purchased home."

— *M & K*
Auburn, CA

POTATO PUDDING WITH SUN-DRIED TOMATOES

Preheat oven to 350 degrees.

2 LARGE ONIONS, *diced*

4 CUPS NEW POTATOES, *diced*

¼ CUP GREEN ONIONS, *chopped*

4 EGGS

1 CUP FLOUR

1 TEASPOON BAKING POWDER

4 TABLESPOONS SUN-DRIED
  TOMATOES, *diced*

SOUR CREAM

*"Our first time in Mendocino, a gem, and
so is your Inn!"*

-J & R
New York City

Place onions and potatoes in food processor and blend until fine. Add eggs and blend well. Add flour and baking powder and blend until smooth. Then add sun-dried tomatoes and blend.

Pour mixture into oiled 9x13 inch baking dish. Bake for 50 minutes. Remove from oven, cool slightly and slice into 8 portions. Serve with sour cream.

Serves 8.

Red Pepper & Mushroom Quiche

Preheat oven to 350 degrees.

14 ounces frozen shredded potatoes
salt & pepper to taste

1 ½ cups milk
4 eggs, *beaten well*
¼ teaspoon nutmeg
salt to taste

⅓ pound mushrooms, *sliced thinly*
½ cup leeks or green onions, *diced*
1 small red bell pepper,
  sliced in 1/4 inch strips
¼ pound pepper jack cheese, *grated*

Oil one glass pie pan and placed potatoes on bottom. Season with salt and pepper and place in 350 degree oven for 20-25 minutes until slightly browned. Remove from oven and shape to bottom and sides of pan. Spread cheese over bottom of pie shell. Sauté onions and mushrooms in a little oil. Distribute over cheese. Place sliced red peppers over mushrooms and onions. Finally, combine milk, eggs, nutmeg, and salt and pour into the shells.

Bake for about 45-60 minutes or until custard is set and the top is puffed and brown. Serve hot, warm or at room temperature.

Serves 10-12.

"Breakfast is out of this world -save room!"

-C &M
California

HORSEBACK RIDING

How would you like to ride a beautiful horse along a Mendocino Coast beach and into a redwood forest? Ricochet Ridge Ranch, just north of Fort Bragg, offers daily trail rides to Mendocino visitors. Lari Shea, a champion horse trainer and mother of two, cares for a string of 80 horses, including some rare Russian Orlovs, and introduces both novice and expert riders to equestrian delights on the Mendocino Coast. Ricochet Ridge Ranch's huge string can accommodate 6-year old children with comfortable ponies, or mount adult first-time riders on docile beasts that walk placidly when and wherever they're told. The Ranch is near MacKerricher State Park, at the south end of Ten Mile beach—a swath of surf-pounded sand that arcs north to Ten Mile River. It's one of the few places in the world where you can live the fantasy of cantering past crashing waves toward a misty horizon while a freshening sea breeze tosses your horse's mane. Shea's amicable relations with timber company Georgia-Pacific, as well as local lodge owners and ranchers, gains her entry to the green coastal hills that ride above the beach and roll inland. Shea is a naturalist at heart and full of wonderful stories about coastal history. Of course, she also has many horse stories to share. The ranch thrives during the busy summer season, and the well-trained and highly experienced staff will lead you on a private or group ride along the beach and through groves of redwood and iris. Choose between English and Western riding styles.

Smokey Cheese & Asparagus Quiche

Preheat oven to 350 degrees.

CRUST:

½ CUP BAKING MIX

2 EGGS

½ CUP MILK

½ CUP GREEN ONIONS, *minced*

FILLING:

4 OUNCES CREAM CHEESE

4 EGGS

1 CUP COTTAGE CHEESE

½ CUP GREEN ONIONS, *minced*

¼ POUND MUSHROOMS, *sliced*

½ CUP BROCCOLI, *finely chopped*

1 BUNCH FRESH SPINACH, *chopped*

¼ CUP FETA CHEESE

¼ CUP SMOKED MOZZARELLA, *grated*

¼ CUP ASIAGO CHEESE, *grated*

¼ CUP SWEET RED PEPPERS

½ CUP ASPARAGUS TIPS,
   lightly steamed

½ CUP FRESH HERBS, *chopped*

Mix crust ingredients together and spread in an oiled 9x11 inch baking dish. Dot with cream cheese. Beat eggs together and add cottage cheese. Sauté green onions, mushrooms, broccoli and spinach until tender. Add to egg mixture with 1/4 cup of the herbs. Pour carefully over crust. Sprinkle cheeses over filling and top with remaining herbs. Slice peppers and arrange over top with asparagus pieces.

Bake for 15 minutes on center shelf then 20-30 minutes on top shelf, until golden brown and puffed.

Serves 10.

SOUTHWESTERN FRITTATA

Prepare at least eight hours in advance.

12 CORN TORTILLAS
14 OUNCES GREEN CHILIES, *diced*
3 CUPS PEPPER JACK CHEESE, *grated*
1 CUP ONION, *chopped*
2 CLOVES GARLIC, *minced*
4 MEDIUM TOMATOES, *diced*

10 EGGS, *beaten*
¾ CUP MILK
½ TEASPOON CUMIN
1 ½ TEASPOONS SALT
½ TEASPOON BLACK PEPPER

PAPRIKA

Lightly oil a 9x13 inch baking dish. Mix onion and garlic with cheese. Spread 1/3 of the chilies over the bottom of pan and 1/3 of the tomatoes. Top with 4 tortillas, torn into one-inch strips. Cover with one cup of cheese mixture. Repeat layering until ingredients are used up. Whisk eggs and milk together and add all spices except paprika. Slowly pour egg mixture over top layer of frittata. Sprinkle with paprika. Cover with foil and refrigerate overnight.

The next day, preheat oven to 350 degrees. Remove foil and bake frittata for 45 minutes until lightly browned and bubbly.

Serves 8-10.

This frittata is based on a recipe from our friends at Skyridge Inn in Torey, Utah at the entrance to Capitol Reef National Park.

Summer Veggie Pie

Vegan (no dairy, no eggs)

13 OUNCES FROZEN POTATOS, *shredded*
SALT AND PEPPER TO TASTE

½ CUP GREEN ONIONS, *chopped*
1 LARGE ONION, *sliced thinly*
1 TEASPOON GARLIC, *minced*
1 TABLESPOON OIL
¾ CUP BROCCOLI, *chopped*
1 CUP ZUCCHINI, *sliced*
1 ½ CUPS MUSHROOMS, *sliced thinly*

1 POUND EXTRA FIRM TOFU, *drained*
2 TABLESPOONS OIL
2 TABLESPOONS LEMON JUICE
½ TEASPOON CRUSHED GARLIC
1 TEASPOON SALT
3 TABLESPOONS FLOUR

PAPRIKA

Vegan?

More and more often these days we have guests who, for health or ethical reasons, are abstaining from animal products. We've been very careful to eliminate meat from all of our dishes, but this request is a little more challenging since we rely so much on milk and eggs in our recipes, especially for the quiches. Luckily Sydney, one of our innkeepers, is an aspiring Vegan and created this quiche from her collection of vegetarian cookbooks. She was a little nervous the first time we served the quiche to a full house, but we didn't let the guests in on the secret ingredient–tofu–until after they had happily polished off the last piece and were raving about how delicious it was. And in fact, no on really minded that they had just been tricked into eating tofu. Looks like the times are truly a-changin'. (The guests who had requested no dairy or eggs really loved this tangy, light but filling dish too!)

Oil a glass pie plate and distribute potatoes over bottom of pan. Bake for 20-25 minutes at 350 degrees, stirring occasionally, until slightly browned. Spread softened potatoes evenly over bottom and sides of pans.

Sauté green onions, yellow onions and garlic in oil until tender. Add broccoli, zucchini and mushrooms and sauté until tender. Drain and place in a large mixing bowl. Set aside.

In a food processor, blend tofu, oil, lemon juice, garlic, salt and flour until very smooth. Add to vegetable mixture and stir. Spread mixture evenly into the pie pans. Sprinkle top with paprika. Bake at 350 degrees for 45 minutes until firm and lightly browned on top.

Serves 10-12.

2 POUNDS NEW POTATOES

½ CUP SUN-DRIED TOMATOES, *chopped*

¾ CUP GREEN ONIONS, *chopped*

1 TEASPOON GARLIC, *minced*

⅛ CUP VEGETABLE OIL
or if the tomatoes are marinated in oil, use 1/8 cup of the marinade

SALT AND PEPPER TO TASTE

¼ CUP CHEDDAR OR PEPPER JACK
CHEESE, *shredded*

"We arrived in a fog and left in a fog. But through champagne and old ghosts we got a magnificent view of each other. Here's to more quiet rooms and glowing embers and honeymoons by the sea."

-D & J

Steam or microwave the potatoes until tender but still holding their shape. While the potatoes are cooking, sauté sun-dried tomatoes, green onions and garlic in the oil until onions are tender. When potatoes are ready, dice and add to the pan. Sauté until potatoes are evenly coated to brown. Season with salt and pepper and any other spices you desire. Transfer to a lightly greased baking dish. Sprinkle with cheese and broil until lightly browned and bubbly.

Serves 8-10.

Toasted Almond Zucchini Quiche

Preheat oven to 350 degrees.

12 OUNCES FROZEN SHREDDED
   POTATOES
SALT & PEPPER TO TASTE
½ CUP JACK, MOZZARELLA, *shredded*
   OR SWISS CHEESE *regular or low fat*

2 CUPS ZUCCHINI, *sliced*
1 CUP MUSHROOMS, *sliced*
½ CUP GREEN ONIONS, *chopped*
1 TEASPOON GARLIC, *minced*
1 TABLESPOON OIL
COOKING SHERRY TO TASTE

2 WHOLE EGGS AND 3 EGG WHITES
1 CUP SKIM MILK
½ CUP LOW FAT SOUR CREAM
¼ TEASPOON SALT
¼ TEASPOON DRY MUSTARD

¼ CUP TOASTED ALMONDS
1 ROMA TOMATO, *sliced*

*When you're thinking of something
a bit on the lighter side, this is one
recipe that you may choose to create.
We've reduced the calories for you,
so just prepare and enjoy!*

Lightly oil one pie plate and line with shredded potatoes. Sprinkle with salt and pepper. Bake for 20 to 25 minutes, stirring occasionally, until lightly browned. Remove from oven and shape to pie plate. Sprinkle cheese over potato crust and set aside.

Sauté zucchini, mushrooms, green onions, and garlic in the oil. Add sherry half way through and sauté until alcohol is just evaporated. Arrange vegetables over cheese. Beat together eggs, milk, sour cream, salt and dry mustard until there are no lumps. Pour gently over vegetables. Decorate with tomatoes and sprinkle with toasted almonds.

Bake for 40-50 minutes until center is set.

Serves 10-12.

TOMATO BASIL TART

Preheat oven to 350 degrees.

ONE PREPARED PIE CRUST, *bottom only*

4 LARGE TOMATOES, *sliced 1/3 inch thick*
½ TEASPOON SALT
¼ TEASPOON PEPPER
1 CUP FRESH BASIL LEAVES
¾ CUP RICOTTA OR COTTAGE CHEESE
4 LARGE EGGS, *beaten lightly*
¼ POUND MOZZARELLA, *grated*
½ CUP PARMESAN CHEESE
SALT AND PEPPER TO TASTE
NON-STICK COOKING SPRAY

Press crust into an oiled tart pan or glass pie plate. Sprinkle tomatoes with salt and let drain on paper towels. In food processor, puree basil with ricotta or cottage cheese. Add eggs and blend. Add mozzarella, Parmesan, salt and pepper and combine. Line bottom of shell with tomato end pieces and spoon cheese mixture over the top. Arrange tomato slices in one layer overlapping them slightly, over the cheese mixture. Spray lightly with non-stick spray.

Bake for 40 minutes or until set. Garnish with basil sprigs, serve hot or at room temperature.

Serves 6-8.

"We have been at your Inn several times. I really love it. I like the atmosphere of the whole town."
                              -K.H.

Running & Hiking

I've been running for twenty years. I'm not fast nor competitive; I run because it provides me peace of mind and good exercise. I have the good fortune to be able to run in Mendocino now—it certainly beats the predawn wintertime runs in Golden Gate Park before heading downtown to the financial district! I thought I'd share a few of my favorite runs with you so that you may start 'psyching up' for a pleasant run or hike on your next visit to a truly remarkable place.
- Jim

Mendocino Headlands State Park

This is my most routine run because it's right in the village. Go down behind the old Presbyterian Church through the parking lot to the gravel path. When you reach the stairs to the beach, turn to the right and follow the path along the rugged headland cliffs past Portuguese Beach, the southwestern point, and up along Heeser Drive to Lansing Street, then right down Lansing to the village. It's about a three mile run on a flat, hard packed gravel and dirt trail. A slight climb at the end to Lansing. For a longer run, reverse direction at the end, and you'll be treated to some wonderful vistas not evident in the other direction.

Fern Canyon, Van Damme State Park

Park your car at the beach lot, cross Highway One and enter the campground, following the low road to the head of the trail, which meanders back and forth across Little River which is really just a creek. Enjoy the lush canyon replete with towering moss-covered redwoods, ferns, and indigenous rhododendrons. Up and back is about five miles. You'll get a bit of a workout on the way up. For you marathon types, you can continue at the end of the trail up the very steep fire road the the Pygmy Forest. Now that's a real workout!

Big River Haul Road

This undulating gravel road, a quarter mile from JGI, goes back at least fifteen miles along Big River which is a tidal estuary for the first six miles. Check with us to make sure the logging trucks are not operating before you set out. It's a pleasant and beautiful run.

Zucchini & Carrot Quiche

Preheat oven to 350 degrees.

13 OUNCES SHREDDED FROZEN
  POTATOES
SALT AND PEPPER TO TASTE

FOR THE FILLING:
½ POUND ZUCCHINI, *grated*
½ POUND CARROTS, *grated*
½ MEDIUM YELLOW ONION,
  sliced thinly
¼ POUND MOZZARELLA CHEESE,
  grated
¼ POUND CHEDDAR CHEESE, *grated*

FOR THE CUSTARD:
1 ¾ CUPS HALF AND HALF
4 EGGS
½ TEASPOON NUTMEG
SALT AND PEPPER TO TASTE

Oil one medium pie plate, place frozen potatoes in plate and toss with salt and pepper. Bake for 20 minutes until lightly browned. Remove from oven and spread potatoes evenly over bottom and sides of pan. Set aside.

Sauté zucchini, onion and carrots in a small amount of oil. Place cheese on bottom of pie shells. Distribute zucchini, carrot and onion mixture over cheese. Beat together custard ingredients and pour over vegetables.

Bake for about 45-60 minutes or until custard is set and the top is puffed and brown. Serve hot, warm or at room temperature.

Serves 10.

Zucchini Parmesan Quiche

Preheat oven to 350 degrees.

FOR ONE 9-INCH POTATO CRUST:
13 OUNCES FROZEN SHREDDED
   POTATOES
SALT AND PEPPER TO TASTE
¼ CUP PARMESAN CHEESE, *shredded*
¼ CUP MOZZARELLA OR JACK
CHEESE, *shredded*

2 CLOVES GARLIC, *minced*
½ CUP GREEN ONIONS, *chopped*
½ TABLESPOON BUTTER
¾ CUP MUSHROOMS, *sliced*
1 ¼ CUPS ZUCCHINI, *sliced*
FRESH BASIL IF AVAILABLE

3 WHOLE EGGS
2 EGG WHITES
1 CUP LOW-FAT MILK
¼ TEASPOON SALT
¼ TEASPOON SUGAR
¼ TEASPOON DRY MUSTARD

1 ROMA TOMATO, *or red pepper, sliced*

¼ CUP PARMESAN CHEESE, *shredded*

Oil pie plate and distribute potatoes over the bottom. Season with salt and pepper and bake for 20-25 minutes stirring occasionally, until lightly browned on top. Remove from oven and shape potatoes to bottom and sides of pan. Place both cheeses on top of crust. Sauté garlic and onions in butter, adding sliced mushrooms and zucchini halfway through. Lightly sauté vegetables (optional: add a shot of sherry to vegetables while sautéing). Add chopped basil and arrange on top of cheese in pie pans.

Beat together eggs, milk, salt, sugar, and mustard and gently pour over vegetables. Top with Roma tomatoes or red peppers. Sprinkle ⅛ cup shredded Parmesan cheese on top. Bake for 40-45 minutes or until center is firm to the touch. Sprinkle remaining cheese over the top while the quiche is hot out of the oven.

Serves 10-12.

SPINACH MUSHROOM PESTO QUICHE

Preheat oven to 350 degrees.

½ CUP POLENTA
1 ½ CUPS WATER
¼ CUP PARMESAN CHEESE
½ TEASPOON SALT

1 LARGE TABLESPOON PESTO
1 CUP MOZZARELLA, *shredded*

1 CUP MUSHROOMS, *sliced thinly*
3 CLOVES GARLIC, *minced*
¼ CUP SUN-DRIED TOMATOES, *chopped*

3 EGGS, *beaten*
1 ¼ CUPS MILK
½ CUP COTTAGE CHEESE
5 OUNCES FROZEN SPINACH,
    thawed with liquid squeezed out

¼ CUP PARMESAN CHEESE, *grated*
1 ROMA TOMATO, *sliced thinly*

*Also known as the "pizza quiche",
this rich and flavorful dish also makes
a tasty dinner entrée served with a
fresh green salad.*

Lightly oil the bottom of one pie plate. In small sauce pan, mix water and polenta and bring to a boil. Reduce heat and stir until thickened. Add Parmesan and salt and mix well. Pour into pie plate covering bottom. Let cool until solidified, about 5-10 minutes. Spread pesto over polenta and sprinkle with mozzarella.

Sauté mushrooms, garlic and sun-dried tomatoes. Beat together eggs, milk and cottage cheese. Add sautéed mushroom mixture and spinach. Mix well. Pour into pie plate. Top with Parmesan and decorate with tomato slices.

Bake for 45 minutes until center is set.

Serves 10-12.

BOTANICAL GARDENS

The mild winters, cool summers, abundant water and the sheltering pine forests of the Mendocino Coast have created one of the finest growing areas in the world. The Mendocino Coast Botanical Gardens was founded in 1961 by Ernest Schoefer, a retired nurseryman, who purchased this property after a year of searching for the ideal location. He and his wife, Betty, began the arduous task of clearing, planting and trail building. They supported the project with a gift shop, a retail nursery and $1 admission. By 1992, the Mendocino Coast Recreation and Park District was able to purchase the entire property with grants from the California State Coastal Conservancy for use as a public botanical garden. The Gardens are now a non-profit organization supported entirely by admissions, memberships, donations, nursery and stores sales and the dedicated work of more than 100 volunteers.

The 47 acre garden boasts more than 20 sizeable collections of plants. These include camellias, dahlias, fushcias, grasses, ivies, heathers, heritage roses, Pacifica iris, perennials, succulents, Mediterraneans, dwarf conifers and a large collection of rhododendron species. The property is sheltered by a native coastal pine forest and includes the fern-covered canyon of Digger Creek, coastal bluffs, and a rocky intertidal habitat. A walk through the gardens takes you through several distinct ecological zones which are wonderfully evident in the changing species of flowers, trees and types of soil. The gardens also offer fantastic wildlife viewing. More than 80 species of birds live in or visit the gardens during the year. Gray whales can be seen during their winter and spring migration and seals sometimes rest offshore on rocks. Trout, frogs, newts and salamanders inhabit Digger Creek and butterflies thrive in the perennial and dahlias gardens.

The gardens are open year-round for self-guided tours, but many workshops and events are held on a regular basis, including a weekly bird walk, gardening and wreath-making classes. The Gardens are the site of the annual late summer "Art in the Gardens", a day-long fundraising art sale featuring fine Mendocino County wines, food and jazz. Winesong!, a benefit for the hospital, is also held at the Gardens. Located just eight miles north of Mendocino off Highway One, the Botanical Gardens make a nice afternoon outing any time of the year!

MEET SYBIL AND BASIL

chapter three

THE REAL OWNERS OF THE INN

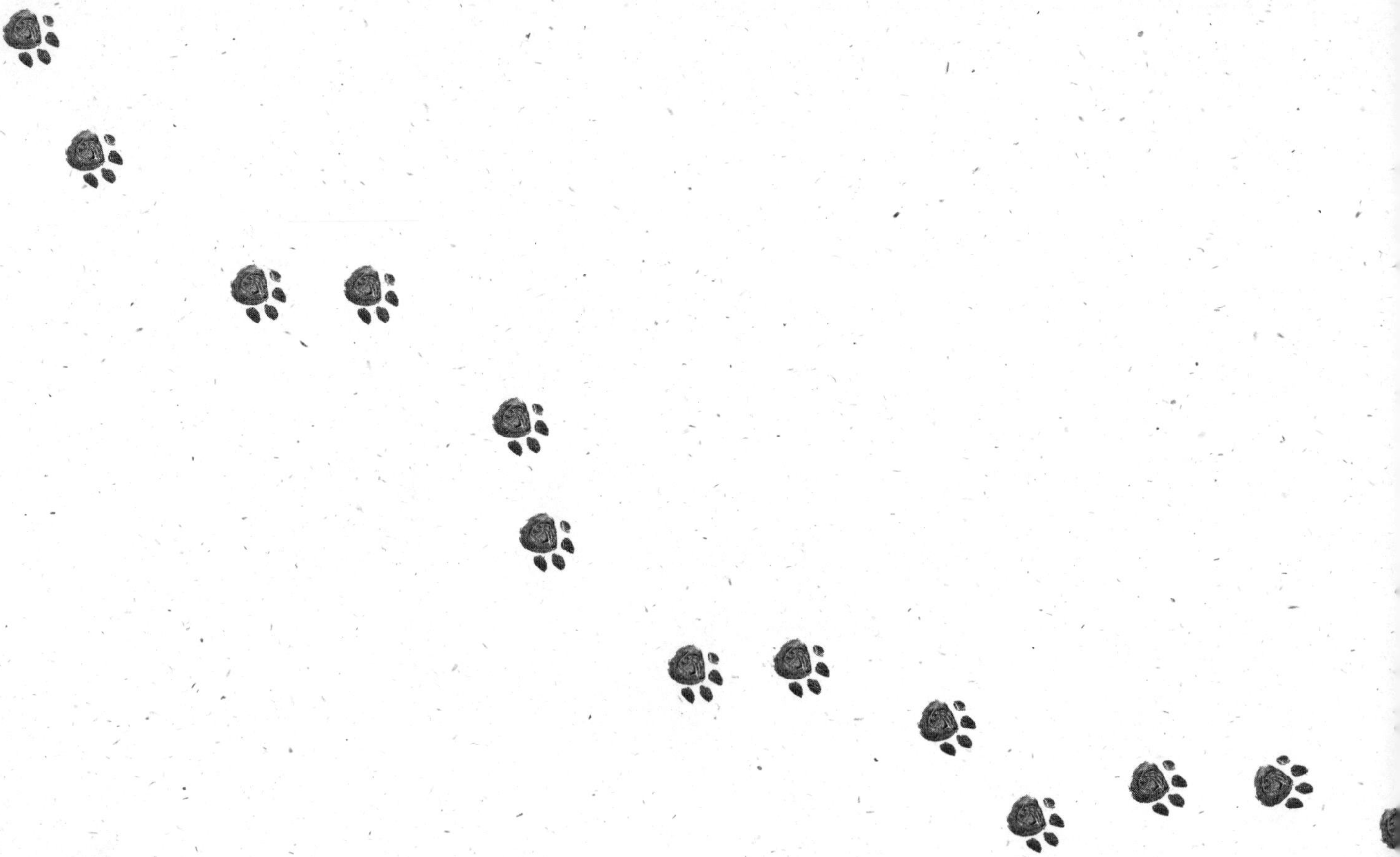

MEET SYBIL & BASIL

We'd like to let you in on a little secret, just between you guests and us cats. Jim and Arlene may think they are the owners of the Inn, but we're really the ones running this place. I'm Sybil, the full-figured Blue-point Siamese with beautiful ice-blue eyes. You could say I'm the boss and Basil is my apprentice. He's still wet behind the ears, really. But let me tell you a little more about myself first. . . One day, back in the fall of 1992, a nice lady named Cookie from the Mendocino Coast Humane Society, brought me to the Inn. She knew that Arlene is a Siamese lover and I fit the bill perfectly. I was just a tiny little sprout then, barely larger than the Inn's coffee mugs, but I was ready for my new job (in the office, check out the photo of me trying to look bigger than a Joshua Grindle Inn coffee mug). Sadie, the Head Inncat at the time, promptly showed me the routine and in no time I was meeting and greeting guests, checking in on them at breakfast and in the parlor during teatime, and schmoozing my way into guests' rooms and warm laps like an old pro. And of course, I immediately set about controlling the gopher population on the front lawn, which had become really out of paw.

When Sadie passed away in the spring of 1995, as much as I missed her warm companionship, I readily marched into the Head Inncat position. It was a lot of extra work, but I take great pride in doing a good job keeping guests happy and I think I was managing pretty well. I knew Arlene was considering adopting another cat, but with her high standards, I felt sure that it would be a long time before she found another feline who could even hold a candle to me. Unfortunately, Sydney, one of the Innkeepers, also works at the Humane Society. One day she spotted Basil waiting to be adopted and Arlene had him here before I even had the chance to meow a protest. You should have seen him. . . a gawky, long legged, pre-teen Chocolate-point Siamese with the most ridiculous looking crossed eyes I had ever seen. I hoped if I ignored him or batted him around enough, he'd get the clue and find another Inn. But he misunderstood all of my efforts as attempts to play, and for the first month that's all he wanted to do. . . PLAY! Well, it took some time but I finally got it into his head that being an Inncat means play comes after work (or sometimes it's one and the same when we provide entertainment for guests). After he settled down a bit and got the excitement of his new-found responsibilities out of his system, he really shaped up to be a decent apprentice. And I was able to cut him a break when I realized that Sadie had to go through the same thing with me at first (although I doubt I was ever as silly as Basil).

As I write this, I'm watching him hunt gophers on the front lawn. Don't tell him I said this, but he has actually taught me a thing or two about the need for agility in hunting, and I'm working on losing some weight so I can keep up with him. (It seems the only growing he's done in the last six months is in his legs and tail!) In fact, I think we make quite a nice pair after all. . . his youth, playfulness and ostentatious displays of affection to guests balance out my wisdom, suave mannerisms, and ability to run an Inn properly. After all, Inncatting is not all about getting snuggles and chasing field rodents; someone has to keep this place in order! You see, when you peek into the office at night and see us "sleeping" under the lamp on the desk next to the computer, don't let our lazy appearance fool you—we're actually in there processing confirmations, making dinner reservations, creating those interesting newsletters and paying the bills! What then, you may ask, are all of the innkeepers for? Why, to pet us and feed us and most importantly. . . open the doors to let us in and out as we please!

So the next time you're visiting the Joshua Grindle Inn, please keep in mind that if you don't get a chance to see us it's because we're very busy cats! However, we do everything we can to make sure each guest who wants to gets a chance to pet us, and we show them how to purrfectly relax, the Mendocino way!

Keep in mind that while we're lucky enough to find such a wonderful home, there are many more cats and dogs still waiting at the shelter for their chance. The Humane Society holds a Pet Adoption Fair every Saturday and Sunday out on the Headlands right next to the Ford House Museum. While you're strolling around town, stop by and give a cat a hug or take a dog for a walk. Even better yet, adopt one of these loving animals and bring him or her home as the ultimate souvenir of Mendocino. The Humane Society will be glad to make arrangements so that you can pick up your new friend on your way out of town, so you don't have to worry about where you'll keep him or her until you depart.

Ah. . . muffins! What a great little package of goodness sitting in your hand. They can be sweet, crunchy, chewy, savory, light, ample, etc. . . muffins are easy to prepare and so quick from the bowl to oven to mouth! Many of our muffins can be assembled ahead of time and then mixed together in the morning before baking if you have a busy morning schedule. Some of our muffins can even be stored as batter in the refrigerator and made individually whenever you need a muffin fix! Scones are practically a bed and breakfast cornerstone and we offer several of our time-tested favorites—as well as tips we've found for making preparation easier. . . an ice-cream scooper is indispensable for the scone baker! Coffeecakes and nut bread are also tried and true standbys, but you won't find your typical boring banana breads and streusel coffeecakes in here (our cooks are too picky to prepare over-served recipes). Enjoy creating these delicious treats at home. . . you don't have to be on vacation to splurge on a piece of coffeecake or a couple of muffins, after all.

WATER TOWERING TREATS & EXCURSIONS FROM THE INN

chapter four

MUFFINS, SCONES, BISCUITS & BREADS

THE WATER TOWERS OF MENDOCINO

So many guests have inquired about the many water towers in the village that we decided to write about them in our cookbook! Visitors are generally curious about what purpose they served, why they still exist, and what their functions are today.

Originally, the towers held water tanks at an elevation sufficient to provide water pressure for home and business use. A 30-foot tower could supply water at about 15 pounds per square inch, adequate for normal domestic use. Windmills were the source of power to pump the water and were quite effective in this windy coastal location. Later, electric pumps pressurized the water, making both the windmills and the towers obsolete.

Water towers were once abundant in Mendocino, but most of them have disappeared through fire, storm damage, neglect or dismantling. However, current zoning and historic district restrictions provide protection for the remaining towers. In fact, a number of new towers have been built in the last dozen years where the property owner has demonstrated to the Mendocino Historic Review Board and the California Coastal Commission that the new construction is actually a replacement of an original tower that had been removed at some earlier time. Examples include the tower at Joshua Grindle Inn (originally built in 1879, replaced in 1984) Barry Cusick's tower at his home on Pine Street (originally built in 1891, replaced in 1988), and Jennifer Taylor's tower on Little Lake Street west of the Art Center (originally built in 1887, replaced in 1991). Today most of the towers serve residential or business uses, or as overnight accommodations here at the Joshua Grindle Inn.

Another new water tower with an interesting story stands behind the Ford House Museum on Main Street. It was constructed in 1991 along with a beautiful old house on the State Park property as a set for the Julia Roberts film *Dying Young*. The house was dismantled after the filming but the park rangers decided to leave the tower standing!

ALICE'S ENGLISH TEA MUFFINS

Preheat oven to 350 degrees.

1 ½ STICKS BUTTER OR MARGARINE
½ CUP SUGAR
2 EGGS

3 ½ CUPS FLOUR
1 TABLESPOON BAKING POWDER
¾ TEASPOON SALT
⅓ TEASPOON CINNAMON

1 ½ CUPS MILK

1 CUP RAISINS
*soaked for ten minutes in English
or Irish Breakfast tea, then drained*

TOPPING:
¾ CUP BROWN SUGAR
⅓ CUP CHOPPED WALNUTS
½ TABLESPOON CINNAMON

Cream the margarine or butter and sugar with an electric mixer. Add the eggs, one at a time, and mix until well blended.

In a separate bowl, stir the flour, baking powder, salt and cinnamon together. Add this mixture alternately with the milk and beat until smooth. Stir in raisins.

Spoon into oiled muffin tins. Mix together topping ingredients with a fork and top each muffin with 1 teaspoon of the mixture. Bake for 15-20 minutes until tester comes out clean.

Makes 18 muffins.

Note: Batter can be stored in covered container in refrigerator for up to two weeks.

APPLE CHEDDAR MUFFINS

Sugar-free

Preheat oven to 400 degrees.

1 LARGE APPLE
  gala or pippin work well
1 ½ CUPS ALL-PURPOSE FLOUR
¼ CUP DRY ROLLED OATS
2 TEASPOONS BAKING POWDER
½ TEASPOON BAKING SODA
½ TEASPOON SALT

¾ CUP LOW FAT MILK
2 EGGS, *beaten*
¼ CUP BUTTER, *melted*
¾ CUP CHEDDAR CHEESE, *finely grated*

Peel apple and cut into ⅛ inch pieces. Set aside. In a large bowl stir together all dry ingredients and set aside. In another bowl whisk together the milk, eggs and butter. Stir in the apples and cheese. Add to dry ingredients and stir just until blended. Scoop into oiled muffin tin. Bake for 15 to 20 minutes or until toothpick comes out clean. Cool about 3 minutes and remove from tin.

Makes 12 muffins.

"A great place for special memories! What's in my heart does not belong in this book."

-M & M
SF & Indy

Short Drives to Redwood Groves

Heading East

Montgomery Woods State Reserve, a remote and impressive stand of virgin redwoods is 25 miles east of Mendocino. The first stage of the 2 mile loop trail is a little steep. But after ten minutes of vigorous climbing, the trail levels off and follows Montgomery Creek through a most spectacular grove of old-growth redwoods. In the winter and spring there is quite a bit of water here–look for the California newt with its bright orange underside. This grove is relatively unknown; often you won't see another person on your hour-long walk. There is no day-use fee. There are toilets but no drinking water, so be sure to bring plenty of water, especially in summer, when it can be very warm–even among these shady giants.

Heading North

For sheer numbers of trees, driving north toward Eureka along the Avenue of the Giants is the way to go. The Avenue is actually the old two-lane highway which takes you through Humboldt Redwoods State Park and parallels Highway 101, starting north of Garberville. Look for the large signs alongside the road indicating which exits you can take to meander along on the old highway. You have the option of returning to Highway 101 at several points along the way. The Avenue ends just south of Scotia.

Heading South

Save-the-Redwoods League bought an 11 mile stretch of redwoods bordering Highway 128, along the Navarro River 15 minutes south of Mendocino and it is now part of the State Park system. Most of the trees are 125-year old second-growth. They are growing right up to the edge of the highway with their limbs entwined above, earning the name "Tunnel to the Sea". Use the turn-outs to explore down to the river; many of the cars you see parked by the road during the spring belong to steelhead fishermen.

To see old-growth redwoods, the 845-acre Hendy Woods State Park is only a short drive from Highway 128 on the Greenwood Ridge Road. Walk through the Big Hendy Grove on a self-guided loop trail. Eighty acres of virgin redwoods, many 300 feet tall, make this accessible park worth the stop.

Blueberry Buckle Coffee Cake

Preheat oven to 350 degrees.

CAKE:
½ CUP MARGARINE
1 EGG
½ CUP SUGAR
½ CUP WHOLE WHEAT FLOUR
1 ½ CUPS ALL-PURPOSE FLOUR
2 ½ TEASPOONS BAKING POWDER
½ TEASPOON BAKING SODA
½ TEASPOON SALT
¾ CUP BUTTERMILK
2 CUPS BLUEBERRIES

TOPPING:
½ CUP SUGAR
⅓ CUP FLOUR
½ TEASPOON CINNAMON
¼ CUP BUTTER OR MARGARINE, *softened*

For the cake, cream the margarine and sugar in an electric mixer. Add the egg and blend well. In a separate bowl, mix together flours, baking powder, soda and salt. Add to the creamed mixture alternately with the buttermilk and mix until smooth. Gently stir in the blueberries. (It is helpful to coat the blueberries with a little flour before adding to mixture, to prevent the batter from turning grey.) Spread batter into an oiled 9x13 inch pan (it will be stiff).

For the topping, combine sugar, flour and cinnamon. Cut in butter until coarse crumbs are formed. Sprinkle over batter. Bake for 30-35 minutes until tester comes out clean.

Serves 10.

BLUEBERRY COFFEE CAKE SCONES

Preheat oven to 375 degrees.

4 ½ CUPS FLOUR
2 CUPS SUGAR
4 TEASPOONS BAKING POWDER
2 TEASPOONS SALT
1 CUP BUTTER
4 EGGS
1 CUP MILK
2 TEASPOONS VANILLA
1 TEASPOON LEMON PEEL, *grated*
2 ½ CUPS BLUEBERRIES, *fresh or frozen*

CRUMB TOPPING:
1 CUP FLOUR
½ CUP BROWN SUGAR
¼ TEASPOON CINNAMON
½ CUP BUTTER

In a large bowl, stir together the flour, baking powder, and salt. Cut the butter into 1/2 inch cubes and distribute them over the flour mixture. Cut in the butter until the mixture resembles coarse crumbs. In a small bowl, stir together the eggs, milk, vanilla, and lemon peel. Add the egg mixture to the flour mixture and stir to combine. The dough will be sticky. With lightly floured hands, gently knead in the blueberries until evenly distributed.

Lightly oil a circle in the center of two pizza pans. Separate the dough into two equal portions and pat each into a 9-inch diameter circle in the centers of the pans. Sprinkle evenly with topping. With a serrated knife, cut into 8 wedges on each pan.

Bake for 30-35 minutes, until the top is lightly browned and toothpick inserted in the middle comes out clean. Place pans on wire racks and cool for 5 minutes. Then remove scones from pans and place on wire racks to cool. Re-cut wedges before serving.

Makes 16 scones.

Blueberry Ginger Muffins

Preheat oven to 400 degrees.

2 ⅓ CUPS ALL-PURPOSE FLOUR
⅓ TEASPOON BAKING SODA
1 TABLESPOON BAKING POWDER
⅓ TEASPOON SALT
⅓ CUP SUGAR
1 TEASPOON CINNAMON
½ TEASPOON GINGER
1 EGG
1 CUP BUTTERMILK
¼ CUP OIL
⅓ CUP DARK MOLASSES
1 CUP BLUEBERRIES, *fresh or frozen*

Stir together flour, baking powder, baking soda, salt, sugar, cinnamon and ginger. Mix eggs, buttermilk, oil and molasses together well. Add this mixture to dry ingredients. Stir until just moistened. Gently fold in blueberries. Fill greased or paper-lined muffin pans 2/3 full.
Bake for 20 minutes, or until done.

Makes 15 muffins.

CARROT MUFFINS

Preheat oven to 350 degrees.

2 CUPS FLOUR
1 CUP BROWN SUGAR
1 CUP SUGAR
1 TEASPOON BAKING SODA
1 TEASPOON SALT
2 TEASPOONS CINNAMON

1 CUP OIL
4 EGGS, *beaten*
2 CUPS CARROTS, *shredded*
1 CUP CRUSHED PINEAPPLE

Combine flour, brown sugar, sugar, baking soda, salt and cinnamon in a large bowl. Set aside. In a separate bowl, combine oil, eggs, carrots and pineapple. Stir into dry ingredients and mix until just moistened. Spoon into oiled muffin tins and bake for 20-25 minutes or until tester comes out clean.

Makes about 18 muffins.

"Much gratitude for your shelter and sustenance–each honed to a fine degree of perfection!"
-C & K

WINE TASTING

Some of the best wine tasting in Northern California is located just 30-45 minutes away. After passing through a beautiful stretch of redwoods on Highway 128 you'll reach the Anderson Valley. Whether you are wine lovers like us or just enjoy a sip here and there, come explore the region for yourself. The wineries typically found in the Anderson Valley are small, unique and unpretentious. Husch winery is a small, family-run vineyard with wine tasting in their converted chicken coop. Navarro Vineyards also has excellent wine and a great view from their picnic area. For sparkling wine lovers, Scharffenberger Cellars, about 4 miles further east, is the place to stop. Two smaller family-run wineries worth visiting and known for their pinot noirs will require directions since they have no highway signs: Lazy Creek Vineyards and Pepperwood Springs Vineyards.

CINNAMON BLUEBERRY MUFFINS

Preheat oven to 375 degrees.

2 CUPS ALL-PURPOSE FLOUR
½ CUP SUGAR
⅔ TABLESPOON BAKING POWDER
¼ TEASPOON BAKING SODA
⅓ TEASPOON SALT
⅓ TABLESPOON CINNAMON

1 CUP MILK
⅓ CUP BUTTER, *melted*
2 EGGS, *beaten*
¾-1 CUP BLUEBERRIES, *fresh or frozen*
CINNAMON & SUGAR MIXTURE

"Our anniversary and we're spending it at the Joshua Grindle Inn again. As always, everything is perfect"
-P & J
Orinda, CA

Combine all dry ingredients in a large bowl. Whisk together milk, butter, and eggs until smooth. Add liquid mixture to the dry ingredients and stir until just blended. Coat blueberries with a little flour and add to batter. Do not over mix.

Spoon muffin mixture into oiled muffin tins filling each cup about 3/4 full. Top with cinnamon and sugar mixture. Bake 15-20 minutes.

Makes 10-12 muffins.

Cinnamon Bran Muffins

Preheat oven to 350 degrees.

1 BOX BRAN BUDS
2 CUPS BOILING WATER

3 CUPS SUGAR
4 EGGS, *beaten*
1 CUP OIL

5 CUPS FLOUR
1 ½ TEASPOONS CINNAMON
1 ½ TABLESPOONS BAKING SODA
2 TEASPOONS SALT
1 TABLESPOON ORANGE PEEL, *grated*
2 CUPS RAISINS

4 CUPS BUTTERMILK

CINNAMON & SUGAR MIXTURE

This is a large recipe, yielding approximately forty muffins, but it can be kept in a covered container in the refrigerator for several weeks. Anytime you want a delicious, healthy, filling bran muffin, you can just take a couple of scoops out of the batter and you're just fifteen minutes away from a morning, afternoon or evening treat.

In a very large bowl, mix together bran buds and water and let stand for 10 minutes. Mix together sugar, eggs and oil and add to the bran buds. In a separate bowl mix together flour, cinnamon, baking soda, salt, orange peel and raisins. Add to bran mixture alternately with buttermilk until well mixed.

Spoon batter into muffin tins for number desired, sprinkle with cinnamon and sugar mixture. Bake for 15-20 minutes, until tester comes out clean. Serve with honey butter.

Makes 40 muffins.

CINNAMON COTTAGE NUT MUFFINS

Sugar-free

Preheat oven to 375 degrees.

2 CUPS ALL-PURPOSE FLOUR
2 ½ TEASPOONS BAKING POWDER
½ TEASPOON BAKING SODA
½ TEASPOON SALT
1 TEASPOON CINNAMON
½ TEASPOON NUTMEG

1 EGG, *beaten*
1 CUP LOW FAT MILK
¼ CUP BUTTER, *melted*
¾ CUP SMALL CURD COTTAGE CHEESE

We always make every effort we can to accommodate guests' dietary needs and this recipe is a wonderful treat for diabetics and others who can't eat sugary muffins.

In a medium bowl stir together all dry ingredients and set aside. In another bowl stir together egg, milk and butter until smooth. Add the cottage cheese and stir until blended. Add to dry ingredients and stir just until blended. Using an ice cream scoop, scoop into oiled muffin tin. Bake 15 to 20 minutes or until a toothpick comes out clean.

Makes 12-16 muffins.

CRANBERRY ALMOND SCONES

Preheat oven to 425 degrees.

1 EGG
1 ½ CUPS BUTTERMILK
2 TEASPOONS ALMOND EXTRACT

4 CUPS FLOUR
4 TEASPOONS BAKING POWDER
1 TEASPOON BAKING SODA
1 TEASPOON SALT
½ CUP SUGAR
1 ½ CUPS BUTTER
1 CUP TOASTED ALMONDS, *chopped*
1 CUP DRIED CRANBERRIES

½ CUP CREAM
½ CUP SUGAR
¼ CUP SLICED ALMONDS

Beat together egg, buttermilk and extract. Combine flour, baking powder, soda, salt and sugar. Cut in butter until mixture resembles coarse crumbs. Add almonds and cranberries.

Lightly mix the liquid ingredients into the dry ingredients until mixture clings together and forms a soft dough. Turn the dough onto a lightly floured surface and knead gently 5-6 turns. Divide dough in quarters and pat into 1/2-inch thick circles. Cut each into 6 wedges.

Place scones on greased baking sheets. Brush with cream and sprinkle with a small amount of sugar and a few sliced almonds. Bake for 12-15 minutes, until lightly browned. Remove from oven and serve warm.

Makes 24 scones.

These are the perfect scones for any occasion and will impress family and friends.

VanDamme State Park and Pygmy Forest

Located just south of Mendocino in Little River, Van Damme State Park encompasses a beautiful expanse of land stretching from the ocean access at the mouth of Little River, through Fern Canyon and up into the Pygmy Forest. The Fern Canyon Trail is a 5-mile round trip hike which takes you along a lush, forested, fern canyon which follows (and crosses over several times) Little River. For hundreds of thousands of years the stream has been eroding its bed in this narrow, shady canyon. At the present stage in its life it is about 5 miles in length and falls some 600 feet, cutting through successive marine terraces that were developed near the seashore and in turn were uplifted by geologic forces. Today, forests–some tall and stately, others short and stunted–grow on these ancient terraces, protection for the slopes below.

The trail is certainly a delight for nature lovers and wildflower enthusiasts. On the sloping sides of the canyon grows a climax forest in which coastal redwood and Douglas fir predominate. But thriving along with these giants are bishop pine, grand fir, western hemlock, madrone, tanoak, California nutmeg, and chinquapin. Nestled in the shade beneath the forest canopy, other plants find their suitable growing conditions–rhododendron, huckleberry, salal, trillium, calypso orchid, oxalis, wild ginger and various ferns, mushrooms and mosses. Along the banks of the stream, where it is more sunny and water is plentiful year-round, elderberry, salmonberry, ferns, horse tail, columbines, skunk cabbage, corn lily, inside-out flower and many others thrive beneath the leafy boughs of red alder and willow. Within the stream and on its damp rocks live grasses, sedges, mosses, liverwort and other water-loving plants.

The easternmost point of the loop trail takes you through the Pygmy Forest, and at the end of the spur which leads out to Little River Airport Road, there is a short boardwalk loop trail which teaches the history of the forest at several marked points. The Mendocino or Pygmy Cypress, Cupressus pygmaea, is found only on coastal terraces between Fort Bragg and Anchor Bay. Outside the podzol areas, the tree reaches over a hundred feet tall (like the stand in back of our Inn); in the Pygmy Forest however, a tree with a trunk diameter of 1/4 inch, standing only a foot or so high, may have as many as sixty growth rings. In general, a pygmy cypress with a one-inch trunk diameter is forty or fifty years old–trunk diameter is generally a better measure of age than is height. Some of the trees in the Van Damme Pygmy Forest are undoubtedly over a century old!

BLUEBERRY CORN MUFFINS

Preheat oven to 375 degrees.

1 ½ CUPS CORNMEAL
1 ½ CUPS FLOUR
½ CUP SUGAR
4 TEASPOONS BAKING POWDER
⅓ TEASPOON SALT
1 ½ CUPS BUTTERMILK
½ CUP BUTTER, *melted*
2 EGGS, *beaten*
1 CUP BLUEBERRIES, *fresh or frozen*

These muffins are a perfect balance between wholesome and sweet. They go well with Mexican dishes and are a great accompaniment to your award-winning chili recipe!

"We have had a lovely time. Great room and breakfast. Blueberry corn muffins are impeccable. So are spiced pears, delightful."
-J & C
Bucks County, PA

Combine cornmeal, flour, sugar, baking powder and salt in a large mixing bowl. Make a well in the center.

In a smaller bowl, beat eggs and butter. Add buttermilk and beat until smooth. Pour into dry ingredients and mix until just moistened.

Fold in blueberries just until combined (over mixing will turn the batter blue). Oil muffin tins and fill until 2/3 full.

Bake for 20-25 minutes, until firm and golden.

Makes 18 muffins.

Variation: Try replacing the blueberries with 1 cup chopped green chilies for a spicy treat!

Apple Crisp Muffins

Preheat oven to 375 degrees.

TOPPING:
2 TO 3 APPLES, *30 ½-inch slices*
¼ TEASPOON ALLSPICE
¼ TEASPOON CINNAMON

BATTER:
2 ¾ CUPS FLOUR
¾ CUP OLD-FASHIONED OATS
½ CUP SUGAR
½ CUP BROWN SUGAR
1 TABLESPOON BAKING POWDER
¼ TABLESPOON CINNAMON
½ TEASPOON ALLSPICE
½ TEASPOON BAKING SODA
¼ TEASPOON SALT

3 EGGS
1 ½ CUPS MILK
¼ CUP BUTTER, *melted*

SUGAR IN THE RAW

Mix together apples, allspice, and cinnamon, set aside. Combine flour, oats, sugars, baking powder, cinnamon, allspice, baking soda and salt in a large bowl. In a separate bowl, beat eggs into melted butter. Add milk and mix well.

Stir wet ingredients into dry ingredients until just moistened. Spoon into oiled muffin tins and top each with two slices of apple. Press apple slices lightly into batter. Sprinkle with sugar in the raw and bake for 20 minutes or until a toothpick comes out clean.

Makes 12 to 15 muffins.

CRANBERRY ORANGE MUFFINS

Preheat oven to 375 degrees.

2 CUPS FLOUR
⅔ CUP SUGAR
¾ TABLESPOON BAKING POWDER
⅓ TEASPOON SALT

5 TABLESPOONS BUTTER, *melted*
⅔ CUP ORANGE JUICE
3 EGGS
1 TABLESPOON ORANGE PEEL, *grated*

⅓ CUP DRIED CRANBERRIES
  or 6 oz. fresh cranberries
11 OUNCES MANDARIN ORANGES

If using dried cranberries, soak overnight in juice from mandarin oranges.

Combine dry ingredients.

Melt butter and whisk eggs. Stir in orange juice and orange peel and beat well. Stir liquid into dry ingredients and mix until just moistened. Add drained cranberries and mandarin oranges. Spoon into oiled muffin tin and bake 15-20 minutes until firm and golden.

Makes 10-12 muffins.

MARION'S CURRANT SCONES

Preheat oven to 350 degrees.

2 ½ CUPS WHITE FLOUR
1 CUP WHOLE WHEAT FLOUR
1 ¼ TABLESPOONS BAKING POWDER
½ POUND BUTTER, *at room temperature*
½ CUP SUGAR
3 LARGE EGGS
½ CUP BUTTERMILK
½ CUP DRIED CURRANTS
½ TABLESPOON DRIED ORANGE
PEEL, *grated*

Based on an original Old English scone recipe by our friend Marion, at the lovely John Dougherty House in Mendocino.

Cream butter and sugar until pale and fluffy. Add eggs, one at a time, beating after each addition. In a separate bowl, mix together flour and baking powder. Add to creamed mixture alternately with buttermilk. Mix until well blended. Fold in currants and orange peel.

Scoop batter with a large ice cream scoop onto ungreased cookie sheet. Bake for 15 minutes until lightly browned. Remove from cookie sheet and cool on wire rack.

Makes 15 scones.

Note: Dough can be prepared and scooped the night before if kept covered on cookie sheets in the refrigerator. Dough can also be frozen in individual servings.

RUSSIAN GULCH STATE PARK

Russian Gulch is a picturesque North Coast Park, whether it be for a picnic, hike or just to have a look. Only 2 miles north of Mendocino, the park offers both the serenity of redwood groves and the excitement of an ocean shore. Though cold, the beach is suitable for swimming and sunbathing, and is also used as an entry point for skin divers. The headland offers a wonderful view of the coast, both north and south, as well as Russian Gulch itself. Out on the headland is a spectacular point of interest, the Devil's Punch Bowl—a sea-cut tunnel about two hundred feet long that has collapsed at its inland end to make a hole a hundred feet across and sixty feet deep. Its steep walls are lined with wildflowers and other small plants. This is one of Mendocino coast's "blowholes." Waves can be seen coming in through the tunnel, but the bowl is too broad and open for any "blowing" effect to be noticeable except under storm conditions.

Inland, the park includes nearly three miles of the heavily forested Russian Gulch Creek Canyon. You can have an afternoon picnic or barbecue with the crashing waves and Mendocino Headlands for a backdrop, or take a stroll down to the beach. A scenic bicycle path makes it easy to see the lower part of the canyon, and a hiking trail continues inland past a beautiful waterfall and up onto the surrounding ridges. If you like to walk in the woods, there are several trails of varying lengths you can try. Whether you hike the 6 1/2 mile round trip, the 7 ½ mile semi-loop or just the first 5 miles round trip (paved road), you are bound to enjoy this heavily forested creek canyon. You may even wish to take a longer hike by connecting some of these trails—for instance, you can take the South Trail from the group camp, then continue up the Canyon Bike Trail and around the Falls Loop Trail, and finally return to camp via the North Trail. In this 3-4 hour hike, which covers over nine miles, you will pass through six different biotic communities. The park entrance is located on the west side of Highway One, just two miles north of Mendocino.

DRUNKEN BANANA BREAD

Preheat oven to 350 degrees.

1 ¼ CUPS WHOLE WHEAT FLOUR
1 TEASPOON BAKING POWDER
½ TEASPOON SALT
½ CUP BUTTER
1 CUP BROWN SUGAR
1 CUP BANANAS, *mashed*
2 EGGS
⅓ CUP CREAM SHERRY
½ CUP CHOPPED WALNUTS

Sherry makes an interesting alteration in flavor for the all-too-common banana bread loaf. This bread is great in the morning, but even better at teatime. Be sure to use a quality drinking sherry rather than cooking sherry.

Oil and flour one medium loaf pan. Combine flour, baking powder and salt and set aside. In a larger bowl, cream butter and sugar, then add eggs, mashed bananas and 1/4 cup of the sherry. Gradually add the dry ingredients, stirring until just blended. Stir in chopped walnuts.

Spread evenly into prepared pan. Bake 55-60 minutes until center tests done. Remove from oven and place on wire rack. Drizzle remaining sherry over the top. Cool for 10 minutes, then remove from pan and place upside down on cooling rack.

Serves 10-12.

Eileen's Irish Soda Bread

Preheat oven to 350 degrees.

3 CUPS FLOUR

⅔ CUP SUGAR

1 TEASPOON BAKING SODA

1 TEASPOON BAKING POWDER

1 TABLESPOON CARAWAY SEEDS

1 ½ CUPS CURRANTS AND RAISINS

2 EGGS, *beaten*

1 ¾ CUPS BUTTERMILK

2 TABLESPOONS BUTTER, *melted*

1 TEASPOON SALT

Combine flour, sugar, baking powder, soda and salt. Stir in currants and raisins. Combine beaten eggs, buttermilk and melted butter. Add to the dry ingredients and mix just until flour is moistened. Turn batter into oiled and floured medium-size loaf pan. Bake for one hour 15 minutes. Remove from pan immediately. Allow to cool before slicing.

Serves 10-12.

Jim's mom, Eileen, brought this recipe with her when she immigrated from Ireland. Eileen bakes this traditional Irish bread for our guests each Thanksgiving.

RASPBERRY MUFFINS

Preheat oven to 375 degrees.

2 ½ CUPS FLOUR
¼ CUP SUGAR
¼ CUP PACKED BROWN SUGAR
1 TABLESPOON PLUS 1 TEASPOON
  BAKING POWDER
½ TEASPOON CINNAMON

2 EGGS, *lightly beaten*
1 CUP MILK
½ CUP BUTTER OR MARGARINE, *melted*

6 OUNCES RASPBERRIES, *fresh or frozen*

TOPPING:
½ CUP WALNUTS, *chopped*
1 CUP PACKED BROWN SUGAR
½ CUP FLOUR
1 TABLESPOON ORANGE PEEL, *grated*
½ TABLESPOON CINNAMON

"The room, the fire, the town. . .
everything was great! But could we
have a dozen muffins—to go, please?"
      -S & E

In a large bowl, mix together flour, sugar, brown sugar, baking powder and cinnamon. In another bowl, combine eggs, milk and margarine or butter. Add to dry ingredients and stir until just blended, being careful not to over-mix. Coat raspberries with a small amount of flour and fold into batter. Spoon into muffin tins. Combine topping ingredients and top each muffin with one teaspoon of the mixture. Bake for 20-25 minutes, until tester comes clean.

Makes 15 muffins.

LEMON WALNUT GINGER MUFFINS

Preheat oven to 375 degrees.

PEEL OF 3 THICK PEEL LEMONS, *grated*
OR 1 TABLESPOON DRIED LEMON
   PEEL, *grated*
1 SMALL GINGER ROOT, *peeled and grated*

1 ½ CUPS SUGAR
¾ CUP BUTTER, *softened*
3 EGGS
1 ½ CUPS SOUR CREAM OR YOGURT

1 ½ TEASPOONS POWDERED GINGER
1 ½ TEASPOONS BAKING SODA
½ TEASPOON SALT
3 CUPS FLOUR
1 CUP WALNUTS, *chopped*

Beat lemon peel, grated ginger, sugar and butter until fluffy. Continue beating while adding eggs and sour cream. In a separate bowl, mix together dry ingredients and nuts. All at once, gently fold dry ingredients into egg mixture.

Bake in oiled tins for 20 minutes, or until tester comes out clean.

Makes 18 muffins.

ORANGE POPPY SEED MUFFINS

Preheat oven to 375 degrees.

2 CUPS FLOUR

⅔ CUP SUGAR

¾ TABLESPOON BAKING POWDER

⅓ TEASPOON SALT

⅛ CUP POPPY SEEDS

5 TABLESPOONS BUTTER, *melted*

3 EGGS

⅔ CUP ORANGE JUICE

1 TABLESPOON ORANGE PEEL, *grated*

"Ah distinctly we remember
it was in the month–September
As we watched each dying ember
(In our 'water tower' heater)

We discussed this B & B
One by the name of Joshua G
Lying tranquil by the sea
(There is no place neater)

Moorehead family is our host
On this Mendocino Coast
'Tis the spot we love the most
(Ain't no B & B can beat her!)"
                    -E & C
                    Whittier, CA

Combine dry ingredients. In a separate bowl beat together melted butter and eggs. Add orange juice and orange rind. Beat well. Stir into dry mixture until just moistened. Spoon into muffin pans and bake at 15-20 minutes.

Variation: Add 1/2 cup mandarin orange slices to batter.

Makes 10-15 muffins.

RASPBERRY KUCHEN

Preheat oven to 375 degrees.

2 EGGS, *well beaten*
1 CUP SUGAR
1 CUP MILK
¼ CUP VEGETABLE OIL
2 CUPS ALL-PURPOSE FLOUR
1 ½ TABLESPOONS BAKING POWDER

12 OUNCES FROZEN RASPBERRIES

TOPPING:
¾ CUP ALL-PURPOSE FLOUR
¾ CUP SUGAR
¼ CUP BUTTER
½ CUP COCONUT
½ TEASPOON CINNAMON

In a bowl, combine eggs, sugar, milk, and oil; mix well. In a separate bowl, mix together flour and baking powder; stir into egg mixture. Pour into an oiled 9x13 inch Pyrex pan. Sprinkle raspberries over batter. For topping, in a small bowl, mix flour with sugar. Cut in butter until mixture resembles coarse crumbs, mix in coconut and cinnamon. Sprinkle topping over raspberries.

Bake for 25-30 minutes, until cake tests done. Best served warm.

Serves 10-12.

"We have always enjoyed your warm, friendly hospitality. Of course, the delicious breakfasts too! Our fist visit to the JGI was during the freeze of December 1991. We arrived on a motorcycle, half frozen. Within 10 minutes, we had hot chocolate delivered to our room along with a hair dryer, on loan, to replace the one I'd forgotten. We knew then, there was no better place to stay on the North Coast."

-J & P
Sacramento, CA

ENGLISH BREAD PUDDING

Prepare one full day in advance.

½ LOAF DAY-OLD SOURDOUGH
   BREAD
¾ CUP RAISINS

12 OUNCES CREAM CHEESE
6 EGGS
½ CUP SUGAR
½ TEASPOON NUTMEG
1 TEASPOON VANILLA EXTRACT
½ TEASPOON RUM EXTRACT

½ CUP HALF AND HALF
½ CUP MILK
¼ CUP TOASTED ALMONDS, *sliced*
CINNAMON AND SUGAR, *mixed together*
WARM MAPLE SYRUP

*We usually serve this recipe warm
from the oven, but we've found from
snacking on leftovers that it is also
wonderful cold. We like to use a day-
old loaf of the Cafe Beaujolais
Country Sourdough when we prepare
this recipe!*

Oil a 9x13 inch baking dish. Cut the bread into small cubes and arrange
1/2 of the cubes over the bottom of the pan. Sprinkle with 1/2 of the
raisins. Beat together one egg, the cream cheese, sugar, nutmeg, vanilla
and rum extract and spread over the cubes in the pan. Top with remaining bread cubes and raisins. Beat remaining 5 eggs with the half and half
and milk. Pour over the bread, top with almonds, cinnamon and sugar.
Cover with foil and let stand in refrigerator for at least 24 hours.

Preheat oven to 325 degrees. Bake covered for 45 minutes, then remove
foil and bake for an additional 30 minutes until custard is set in the middle. Cut into squares and serve with warm maple syrup.

Serves 10.

Jughandle Ecological Staircase

The Jughandle Ecological staircase and State Reserve offers a beautiful small beach, many short trails around the ocean cliffs leading down to tidepools, and a 5-mile loop trail called the Ecological Staircase. The trail is essentially a living ecological museum that has evolved over half a million years. It is said to be the longest and most complete record of geologic succession known. Keep your senses piqued to the changing flora, fauna and earth formations as the trail takes you up and across five wave-cut marine terraces pushed up over time as a result of the tremendous tectonic forces that have built the coastal range of mountains. Each "step" of the staircase is about 100 feet higher and 100,000 years older than the next. The youngest terrace emerged from the sea about 100,000 years ago and the oldest terrace is more than 500,000 years old. The trail begins as a short stroll along the headlands then heads down into a creek canyon. As you ascend on the other side, the trail leads east through mixed pine forest and grasslands into a tall, shady forest of Bishop pines, hemlock, fir and spruce. Eventually you will notice the soil turning to orange-brown hardpan while passing through Douglas firs and redwoods. Finally the forest curtain opens dramatically to the flat, sunny ground lined by the "miniature" trees of the Pygmy Forest. As you near the end of the trail, a drainage ditch shows the layers of soil underlying the pygmy bog: thin humus, thick leached pod-sol, reddish brown and iron-rich hardpan, then beach sand and gravel underlaid with graywacke sandstone bedrock. The ditch leads downhill and eventually to a point where it rejoins the main trail back to the first terrace.

The reserve is located 5-10 minutes north of Mendocino on the west side of Highway One. Interpretative brochures outlining 32 marked points along the trail are available for purchase at the trail head.

Fresh Strawberry Muffins

Preheat oven to 375 degrees.

1 ½ CUPS FLOUR
½ CUP SUGAR
¾ TABLESPOON BAKING POWDER
½ TEASPOON SALT
½ TEASPOON BAKING SODA
1 EGG, *slightly beaten*
⅓ TEASPOON ALMOND EXTRACT
¾ CUP BUTTERMILK
⅓ STICK MARGARINE, *melted*
1 CUP FRESH STRAWBERRIES, *chopped*

CINNAMON & SUGAR MIXTURE

"To Us:
Our hearts are happy
Our spirits lifted
Our souls mated
Our room is gifted"
-N & J
Healdsburg

Mix together flour, sugar, baking powder, salt and baking soda. In a separate bowl, beat together eggs, almond extract, buttermilk and margarine. Add buttermilk mixture to dry ingredients and mix until dry ingredients are just moistened. Gently fold in fresh strawberries. Fill oiled muffin tins 2/3 full. Top with cinnamon/sugar mixture. Bake 15 minutes or until tester comes out clean in the middle.

Makes 10-12 muffins.

Sweet Potato Cranberry Muffins

Preheat oven to 375 degrees.

½ CUP BUTTER, *softened*
⅓ CUP LIGHT BROWN SUGAR
4 EGGS, *separated*
2 CUPS MASHED SWEET POTATO,
  cooked & peeled, preferably yams

3 CUPS FLOUR
1 ½ TEASPOONS SALT
2 TABLESPOONS BAKING POWDER
2 TEASPOONS CINNAMON
1 TEASPOON GINGER
½ TEASPOON NUTMEG

1 CUP WALNUTS, HAZELNUTS OR
  PECANS, *chopped*
1 CUP CRANBERRIES, *cut in half*

½ CUP PLUS 3 TABLESPOONS MILK

These muffins are a great accompaniment to any holiday meal–Thanksgiving, Christmas or even Halloween!

In large bowl, cream butter with brown sugar until fluffy. Beat in egg yolks, one at a time. Scrape sides of bowl and add sweet potato. In a separate bowl, sift together flour, salt, baking powder, cinnamon, ginger and nutmeg. Add nuts to dry ingredients. Beat egg whites until stiff.

Add dry ingredients to sweet potato mixture alternately with milk, beginning and ending with dry ingredients. Fold in cranberries and egg whites.

Spoon into oiled muffin tins and bake for 35 minutes or until tester comes out clean.

Makes approximately 15 muffins.

Vegan Cranberry Banana Muffins

No dairy-no eggs

Preheat oven to 350 degrees.

1 ½ TABLESPOONS CORNSTARCH
¾ TABLESPOON BAKING POWDER
⅓ TEASPOON BAKING SODA
2 ⅔ CUPS FLOUR

⅓ CUP MARGARINE
⅓ CUP SUGAR, *optional*
⅓ CUP ORANGE JUICE
1 ½ CUPS BANANAS, *mashed*

⅔ CUP WALNUTS OR PECANS, *chopped*
8 OUNCES WHOLE CRANBERRY SAUCE

"This place is a haven from the unruly, fast paced world."
J & W
-San Jose, CA

Mix together cornstarch, baking powder, soda and flour. Cream together margarine, (sugar), bananas and orange juice. Stir into flour mixture. Fold in nuts and cranberry sauce. Spoon into muffin tins and bake at 350 degrees for 20-25 minutes until lightly browned and tester comes out clean.

Makes 18 muffins.

Maple Corn-Drop Biscuits

Preheat oven to 375 degrees.

1 ½ CUPS CORN MEAL
1 ½ CUPS FLOUR
2 TABLESPOONS BAKING POWDER
½ TEASPOON SALT
⅓ CUP MAPLE SYRUP MIXED WITH
    MILK, *to make 1/2 cup total liquid*
½ CUP BUTTER, *cut into pieces*

Stir together cornmeal, flour, baking powder, and salt in a large bowl. Add butter to the flour mixture and cut in with a pastry blender until mixture resembles coarse crumbs. Add the milk mixture and stir with a fork until a very soft dough forms.

Drop 1/4 cupfuls of dough 2 inches apart onto an ungreased cookie sheet. Bake for 12 minutes, until pale golden brown. Cool on a wire rack.

Makes 12-14 biscuits.

You've just arrived at the Inn after a long day driving through the redwoods and visiting wineries and all you want is a nice, comfortable place to sit down and have a little refreshment. Our parlor is waiting for you stocked with cream sherry, mineral water, a selection of herbal teas, a jar of biscotti, and some devilishly delicious treats arranged on the sideboard. The parlor is a welcome respite in the afternoon for our exhausted guests (shopping and relaxing are hard work!), but it is also a great place to meet the other guests and get to know them. Many evenings we'll go into the parlor to refill the tea water or put out some more goodies and find a group of guests from all over the country—and the world—having conversations about the most interesting things. Sometimes a guest will even experiment with playing the antique pump organ! One of the main things that makes a bed & breakfast inn stand apart from a hotel is the chance to meet and mingle with the other guests in a homey situation which encourages such interaction. This is what makes a stay at a bed & breakfast so special—that feeling that you're visiting a friendly home for the holidays. . . anytime of year! These recipes are easy to prepare, but even easier to devour. Enjoy them with the memories and anticipation of time well spent with new-found friends in the Joshua Grindle parlor!

PARLOR GOODIES AND MENDOCINO SPECIAL EVENTS

chapter five

TREATS FOR AFTERNOON TEA

Mendocino Music Festival

The Mendocino Music Festival presents its annual concert series every July. The classic series, held in the wonderful, gigantic white tent on the Mendocino Headlands, typically includes orchestra and chamber concerts, jazz, an opera, an evening of dance, and more. There are local and visiting artists alike, both professional and amateur, often joining together for different pieces—creating a beautiful patchwork of talent. It is wonderful to see many acclaimed musicians play in such a gorgeous and comfortable setting, and the next to night see shopkeepers and other local faces performing on the stage as well!

The Music Festival is an enormous endeavor. Measuring almost 90 feet wide, the stage and tent are assembled every year and then broken down into sections and stored. The Festival commissions a commemorative poster each year, which is used throughout the promotion and production of the festival. The warm, clear, long July evenings present the perfect backdrop for this two week feast of music.

This is a very big event which often sells out. If you plan on attending, book early! Even if you are unable to get tickets in advance for seating inside, it is a wonderful treat to grab a bottle of wine, a picnic dinner and a warm blanket and sit outside on the Headlands while listening to the musicians play and watching the sun set over the ocean!

Chocolate Biscotti Crunch Cookie

Preheat oven to 350 degrees.

1 cup butter
1 ¾ cups sugar
1 cup small curd cottage cheese
1 teaspoon vanilla extract
2 eggs

2 ½ cups flour
½ cup cocoa
1 teaspoon soda
1 teaspoon baking powder
½ teaspoon salt

2 cups ground biscotti

Here's what to do with all those broken biscotti pieces and crumbs at the bottom of the bag! A delightfully chewy, crunchy cookie!

Cream butter and sugar until fluffy. Add cottage cheese and vanilla and beat well. Add eggs, one at a time, beating well after each addition. Mix together flour, cocoa, soda, baking powder and salt. Gradually add to creamed mixture, mixing well. Fold in biscotti crumbs. Drop by rounded teaspoonfuls onto ungreased cookie sheet and bake for 15 minutes. Let stand a few minutes before moving to cooling rack.

Makes 2 dozen cookies.

CHOCOLATE CHIP TOASTED ALMOND COOKIES

Preheat oven to 350 degrees.

¾ CUP MARGARINE, *softened*
½ CUP SUGAR
1 TEASPOON VANILLA EXTRACT
¼ TEASPOON ALMOND EXTRACT

1 CUP FLOUR
1 CUP SEMISWEET CHOCOLATE CHIPS
1 CUP ALMONDS, *slivered*

This is one of the recipes we serve when folks who don't eat dairy products are staying with us. It's pretty rare to find a cookie recipe that doesn't require an egg or two, but this one is fantastic and very easy!

Cream margarine and sugar together in a medium bowl using an electric mixer set at medium speed. Add extracts and beat well. Add flour, chocolate chips and almonds and blend on low speed until just combined. Place by teaspoonful on ungreased cookie sheet, 2 inches apart. Press with bottom of spoon.

Bake 15-17 minutes or until cookies begin to brown. Remove from oven and transfer to a flat, cool surface.

Makes 2 dozen cookies.

CHOCOLATE ZUCCHINI CAKE

Preheat oven to 350 degrees.

FOR ONE 10-INCH BUNDT CAKE:

¾ CUP BUTTER

2 CUPS SUGAR

3 EGGS

2 TEASPOONS VANILLA

1 TABLESPOON ORANGE PEEL, *grated*

2 CUPS RAW ZUCCHINI, *grated*

2 ¾ CUPS FLOUR

½ CUP COCOA

2 ½ TEASPOONS BAKING POWDER

1 ½ TEASPOONS BAKING SODA

1 TEASPOON SALT

1 TEASPOON CINNAMON

½ CUP LOW FAT MILK

1 CUP WALNUTS, *chopped*

LEMON ORANGE GLAZE:

1 CUP POWDERED SUGAR

1 TABLESPOON VANILLA

2 TEASPOONS ORANGE PEEL, *grated*

LEMON JUICE

This rich chocolaty cake will satisfy that craving in all of us. And because of the added zucchini this is a chocolate cake you can feel good about after you've eaten it. No guilt feelings here!

Grease and flour one bundt pan. Cream butter and slowly add the sugar, beating until smooth. Beat in the eggs and mix thoroughly. Stir in the vanilla, orange peel and grated zucchini and blend well. Mix together the flour, cocoa, baking powder, salt and cinnamon. Add to the zucchini mixture alternately with the milk and beat until thoroughly mixed. Pour batter in prepared pan and bake for 60 minutes, or until a toothpick inserted in center comes out clean.

To make glaze, stir vanilla and orange peel into powdered sugar until a thick paste is formed. Stir in enough lemon juice to make glaze pourable. When cake is completely cooled, turn out of pan onto serving plate and drizzle glaze over the top. Garnish with fresh flowers.

Serves 8-10.

GLAZED CRANBERRY LEMON BREAD

Preheat oven to 350 degrees.

6 TABLESPOONS BUTTER
¾ CUP SUGAR
2 EGGS, *beaten*
2 TEASPOONS LEMON PEEL, *grated*
2 CUPS FLOUR, *sifted*
2 ½ TEASPOONS BAKING POWDER
½ TEASPOON SALT
¾ CUP MILK
1 CUP FRESH OR DRIED
   CRANBERRIES, *chopped*
½ CUP WALNUTS, *chopped*

2 TEASPOONS LEMON JUICE
2 TABLESPOONS SUGAR

Cream together butter and sugar until light and fluffy. Add eggs and lemon peel and beat well. Sift together flour, baking powder and salt, and add to mixture alternately with milk. Beat until smooth after each addition. Stir in cranberries and walnuts.

Pour into oiled medium size loaf pan and bake for 55-60 minutes, or until tester comes out clean. Cool in pan 10 minutes, then remove from pan and cool completely on rack. Combine lemon juice and sugar and spoon over top. Cut into slices and serve.

Serves 10-12.

"Its been some time since my last visit; I have always enjoyed my stay; the Joshua Grindle Inn is one of Mendocino's most charming Bed and Breakfast Inns. The cookbook is a fine way to share all the early morning memories of good food, people and conversation that have always made Mendocino my home away from home."

-V.S.

WINESONG!

Amidst the beautifully landscaped setting of the Mendocino Coast Botanical Gardens, one of the best events on the North Coast, Winesong! combines the pleasures of music, food and wine into a truly memorable afternoon. Approximately thirty restaurants and food merchants and over ninety wineries participate. Music offerings include string quartet, traditional, classical and jazz performances. The highlight of the event is the wine auction which benefits the Mendocino Coast Hospital Foundation. Expect to see a large and impressive array of fine wines offered at the auction. This event is held the first weekend after Labor Day and is always sold out well in advance, so one must plan ahead!

Julie's Carrot Cake

Preheat oven to 350 degrees.

2 CUPS FLOUR

2 TEASPOONS BAKING SODA

1 TEASPOON SALT

2 CUPS SUGAR

I TEASPOON CINNAMON

1 ½ CUPS OIL

4 EGGS

2 CUPS RAW CARROTS, *grated finely*

1 CUP CANNED CRUSHED PINEAPPLE,
   drained

FILLING AND ICING:

16 OUNCES CREAM CHEESE

1 CUP MARGARINE OR BUTTER,
   softened

4 CUPS POWDERED SUGAR

8 OUNCES SHREDDED COCONUT

2 CUPS CHOPPED NUTS

1 TABLESPOON LEMON JUICE

College student Julie Reed, who helps out in the kitchen each summer, contributed this tasty recipe.

Oil and flour two 9-inch round cake pans. Mix together flour, baking soda, salt, sugar and cinnamon. Beat in oil, eggs, carrots and pineapple. Pour into prepared pans and bake for 45 minutes, checking after 25 minutes, until cake springs back when touched.

Cool cakes in pans for 5 minutes, then turn out onto cooling racks. Blend together icing ingredients in order. When cakes are completely cooled, fill and frost with icing. Garnish with flowers and mint sprigs.

Serves 12-14.

Raisin Molasses Drops

Preheat oven to 350 degrees.

¾ CUP BUTTER
1 CUP SUGAR
¼ CUP MOLASSES
1 EGG

2 CUPS FLOUR
2 TEASPOONS BAKING SODA
1 TEASPOON CINNAMON
½ TEASPOON GROUND CLOVES
½ TEASPOON GINGER
¼ TEASPOON SALT

1 CUP RAISINS
SUGAR

Beat the butter and one cup of sugar until light and fluffy. Add molasses and egg; beat well. Combine flour, soda, cinnamon, cloves, ginger and salt. Add to molasses mixture; mix well. Stir in raisins. Cover; refrigerate until chilled. Shape into 1-inch balls; roll each in sugar. Place 2 inches apart on ungreased cookies sheets and flatten with palm. Bake in upper third of oven for 10-12 minutes at 350 degrees. Cool one minute; transfer to wire racks.

Makes about 3 dozen cookies.

"I believe that JGI does truly awaken the senses: I don't know if it's the aroma of the good food after a restful night, the relaxing atmosphere, the sights of the beautiful Mendocino Coast, or the hospitality, or a combination of all of these. What a wonderful way to revitalize and become more aware of the basic elements of life."
-K.G.
Olathe, KS

Orange Chocolate Chip Cookies

¾ CUP SUGAR

¾ CUP BROWN SUGAR

½ CUP BUTTER, *softened*

2 TABLESPOONS OIL

2 TABLESPOONS ORANGE OIL*

2 EGGS

2 CUPS FLOUR

½ CUP WHOLE WHEAT FLOUR

1 TEASPOON BAKING SODA

1 TEASPOON SALT

½ CUP WALNUTS, *chopped*

1 CUP SEMI SWEET CHOCOLATE CHIPS

available at specialty food and cooking supply stores; we like Boyajian from Williams-Sonoma

Cream together the sugars, butter, oil and orange oil. Add the eggs and mix well. Combine the flours, soda and salt. Add to the creamed mixture and blend well. Stir in the nuts and chocolate chips. Drop by rounded tablespoonfuls onto ungreased cookie sheet. Bake for 10 minutes at 350 degrees, or until a light brown color and no longer shiny on top. Be careful not to overbake, as the orange oil burns easily. Let cool on sheet a few minutes before transferring to a cooling rack.

Makes about 3 dozen cookies.

LEMON SQUARES

Preheat oven to 350 degrees

CRUST:
2 ⅔ CUPS FLOUR
½ CUP SUGAR
1 CUP BUTTER, *softened*

FILLING:
1 ½ CUPS SUGAR
4 EGGS
4 TABLESPOONS FLOUR
½ TEASPOON BAKING POWDER
6 TABLESPOONS LEMON JUICE

2 TABLESPOONS POWDERED SUGAR

Blend crust ingredients together with a pastry cutter or two knives and press into a 9x 11 pan. Bake for 15-20 minutes or until slightly browned.

Mix together filling ingredients and pour over crust. Bake an additional 18-20 minutes, until top begins to brown and center is set. Cool completely, then sift powdered sugar over top to finish. Cut into squares.

Makes 1 dozen squares.

An old favorite of many, the lemon squares are always enjoyed by our guests. They are simple to prepare and just the right snack at the end of the evening.

Mendocino Christmas Festival

The Mendocino Christmas festival begins each year with the annual Kelley House Christmas Tree Lighting ceremony on the first Friday in December. This traditional event brings the community out for caroling under the outdoor tree followed by good cheer inside. Santa comes to Kelley House on big red fire truck and delivers gifts to all the children.

The Mendocino Christmas Festival continues through the month with a number of special events:

Sing-Along Messiah

Holiday Gallery Tours

Celebrity Cooks & Kitchens Tour

Christmas Ornament and Wreath Making Party

Entertainment by Dickens Carolers

Musical Stage Productions

Candlelight Inn Tour

One of the most popular events is the Candlelight Tour of the Bed and Breakfast Inns of Mendocino. The innkeepers of Little River and Mendocino welcome you to their beautiful and distinctive inns. The inns are open for touring and light refreshments are served. This is a perfect beginning to the holiday season.

PINEAPPLE CHOCOLATE CAKE

Preheat oven to 350 degrees.

¾ CUP PLUS 2 TABLESPOONS
   BUTTER, *softened*
1 ½ CUPS SUGAR
1 TEASPOON VANILLA
3 EGGS

1 CUP FLOUR
1 TEASPOON BAKING POWDER
½ TEASPOON SALT
½ TEASPOON CINNAMON
8 TABLESPOONS UNSWEETENED
   COCOA POWDER
¼ CUP WALNUTS, *chopped*
1 CUP PINEAPPLE, *drained & crushed*

Cream butter, sugar and vanilla together. Beat in eggs. Mix together flour, baking powder, salt, cinnamon and cocoa powder. Add gradually to creamed mixture and mix thoroughly. Stir in nuts and pineapple.

Pour into a greased 8x10 inch pan and bake for 35-40 minutes, until center tests done. Cool and cut into large squares.

Makes 8-12 pieces.

TURTLE BARS

Preheat oven to 350 degrees.

14 OUNCES CARAMEL CANDIES
⅔ CUP EVAPORATED MILK

1 PACKAGE GERMAN CHOCOLATE
   CAKE MIX
¾ CUP BUTTER, *melted*

1 CUP PECANS, *coarsely chopped*
1 CUP CHOCOLATE CHIPS

"There once were two women on vacation and at the Joshua Grindle they had relaxation.

The food was quite nice with sugar and spice and to return was a tremendous temptation."

Unwrap caramels and melt with 1/3 cup evaporated milk in saucepan over low heat, stirring often.

Mix together cake mix, melted butter and the other 1/3 cup evaporated milk until cake mix is completely moistened. Pour 1/2 batter into a lightly oiled 9x13 inch baking dish and spread evenly. Bake for 6 minutes.

Remove from oven and pour caramel mixture over the top. Sprinkle with pecans and chocolate chips. Dot with remaining cake mixture. Return to oven and bake for 20 minutes longer. Let cool completely, then refrigerate.

Makes 12-18 bars.

PERFORMING ARTS

MENDOCINO THEATRE COMPANY

Incorporated in 1977, MTC has become a key element in the success of cultural development on the North Coast. Originally known as the Mendocino Performing Arts Company (MPAC), its name was changed to Mendocino Theatre Company (MTC) in 1992 to emphasize the point that it has truly developed as a theatre company and that it does not encompass all of the performing arts.

In its first year, the company produced three plays. In 1978 and 1979 five plays were mounted and since then, six Main Stage plays have been produced each year. The plays continue to be carefully selected to offer a cross section of productions, including old favorites, contemporary plays, comedy, drama, and some experimental works. In addition to Main Stage productions, numerous offering by Stage Two, the Reading Series, and special, short-run events such as "A Christmas Carol" have been mounted.

WAREHOUSE REPERTORY THEATRE

This new company, formed in 1995, has impressed audiences with their powerful and inspired performances. Warehouse offers challenging experiences which stretch the mind and introduces audiences to people, emotions and situations foreign to the daily lives of most. Dramas and comedies handling personal and present day topics interspersed with Shakespearean Classics, all professionally acted and directed.

GLORIANA OPERA COMPANY

Living in Mendocino, we are proud to have this opera company with its many talented performers of all ages and backgrounds. The company's performances take place at the Cotton Auditorium in Fort Bragg, and have included such classics as "Man of La Mancha", "Oliver", and "The Sound of Music".

MENDOCINO AND FORT BRAGG WHALE FESTIVAL

Mendocino celebrates the migration of the California Gray Whale each year at its whale festival the first weekend in March. Our many art galleries have special marine exhibits, and if art is not your cup of tea, you can purchase a commemorative wine glass and wander around to the various galleries sampling our fine local wines. Local restaurants provide you with a chance to judge their seafood chowders at the Chowder Cook-off in Crown Hall. The Ford House on Main Street is the Park headquarters and offers visitors films on whales and ranger-led walks on the headlands.

Fort Bragg celebrates its whale festival two weeks later, offering beer tasting from our local micro-breweries, visits to art galleries, a life-size mobile model of a whale that spouts and speaks, and the Whale Run 10K. The run, popular with both serious runners and casual joggers, is held on the old logging road in MacKerricher State Park, just north of Fort Bragg. The view alone is enough to inspire the most dedicated couch potato! If thinking about a 10K run makes you tired, just imagine the gray whales undertaking a 10,000 mile trek–the longest migration of any mammal! Catching a glimpse of these graceful and magnificent creatures as they go by on their journey is truly one of the joys of visiting Mendocino and a true cause for celebration!

We purchased the Inn in May of 1989 after thoroughly researching the business, asking innkeepers for advice, asking ourselves if it 'felt right', and attending an in-depth seminar for prospective innkeepers. One of the topics in the seminar was that of Innkeeper Burnout. Anecdotal research indicates that innkeepers are likely to burn out after five or six years, probably caused by the individuals trying to do it all themselves with little or no staff support.

Those poor innkeepers, we imagined, they just don't know how to organize and manage their business. We won't have that problem, we decided, because of our strong business backgrounds. Those burnout cases were probably not 'real business people' in their prior lives and simply did not have the necessary experience to balance their work with play.

Well, we were wrong! We realized in 1994 that we actually were starting to show signs of burnout. We were working six and seven day weeks and since we lived on the property, we were always confronted with diverse facets of innkeeping, even when we tried to relax.

We decided to seek the advice of successful, long term innkeepers whom we admire. They said that the best solution to burnout is to put some distance between yourself and your inn—both physically and psychologically—by moving off the property. We did just that in the summer of 1995; we purchased a home four miles east of the village on Outlaw Springs Road. Our resident innkeeper now lives in the Bungalow behind the Main House and we are commuters (again).

Although we are probably working nearly as many hours, the pace is much different because when it's time to 'turn off the Inn', we can do it. We are better innkeepers for the move; our positive attitudes inspire our staff to excel in their work. This, in turn, gives a clear message to our valued guests: Joshua Grindle Inn is a good place to stay because the proprietors and staff are enthusiastic about their jobs. Another pleasant stay can be anticipated!

- Jim & Arlene

chapter six

JIM & ARLENE'S FAVORITE DINNER RECIPES

BAKED GOAT CHEESE WITH WATERCRESS & ARUGULA

11 OUNCES GOAT CHEESE, *in a tube*
4 TABLESPOONS OLIVE OIL
½ CUP BREAD CRUMBS

FOR THE DRESSING:
1 CUP OLIVE OIL
⅓ CUP SHERRY VINEGAR
2 CLOVES GARLIC, *minced*
1 TABLESPOON DIJON MUSTARD
¼ TEASPOON SALT
FRESHLY GROUND BLACK PEPPER

WASH AND PAT DRY:
1 BUNCH WATERCRESS
1 BUNCH ARUGULA

SUN-DRIED TOMATO GARNISH

Day before
Spoon olive oil into a small bowl. Put 1/2 cup bread crumbs into another bowl. Cut goat cheese into 12 small rounds (dental floss works well for this). Coat each piece with oil and then bread crumbs. Refrigerate overnight.

Day after
Cut greens into thin strips, toss with dressing. Bake goat cheese slices at 400 degrees until brown and just beginning to soften, about 7 minutes. Divide salad greens around 6 plates, place 2 slices of the warm goat cheese in the center of each plate, garnish with sun-dried tomato slices and serve immediately.

Serves 6.

GARLIC BUTTERMILK MASHED POTATOES

6 POTATOES FOR MASHING
  yellow fin are best

1 HEAD GARLIC

1 TEASPOON OLIVE OIL

BUTTERMILK

SALT AND PEPPER

This recipe delivers all the comfort and taste with very little fat!

Place garlic head on a sheet of foil and drizzle with olive oil. Wrap foil around garlic, place in a small bowl and roast at 400 degrees for one hour. Cut potatoes into cubes and boil until just cooked. Squeeze garlic from skins and mash with potatoes, adding just enough buttermilk to reach desired consistency. Season with salt and pepper.

Serves 4.

HERB CRUSTED ROAST SALMON

Preheat oven to 425 degrees.

4 SALMON FILETS
1 CUP BUTTERMILK

1 CUP SOURDOUGH BREAD CRUMBS
HERBS DE PROVENCE
FRESH GROUND PEPPER

The high temperature seals the buttermilk and crumbs; the salmon stays moist on the inside and crusty on the outside.

Mix herbs and pepper with bread crumbs. Dip salmon in buttermilk and roll in bread crumbs to cover. Place in lightly oiled pan and roast until just done (approximately 12-15 minutes). Serve with Portuguese peas and garlic mashed potatoes.

Serves 4.

LEG OF LAMB MENDOCINO

5 TO 6 POUND LEG OF LAMB
12 CLOVES GARLIC, *slivered*

1 CUP MENDOCINO COUNTY PINOT
   NOIR OR FRUITY ZINFANDEL WINE
1 CUP SOY SAUCE
½ CUP WATER
2 TABLESPOONS BROWN SUGAR
1 LARGE ONION, *chopped*
6 LARGE ROSEMARY SPRIGS
1 TABLESPOON THYME
1 TABLESPOON OREGANO
2 TEASPOONS PEPPER

Bone and butterfly the leg of lamb. Insert garlic into the meat by using a knife tip to puncture the meat then insert garlic slivers into this space. Combine remaining ingredients and marinate overnight, turning occasionally. Barbecue over hot charcoal skin side up (reserve marinade) for 15 minutes. Turn and cook additional 15 minutes or until desired doneness is reached (medium-rare is recommended). Baste occasionally with reserved marinade. Slice across grain in thin slices and serve.

Serves 8-10.

MINNIE'S PORTUGUESE PEAS

12 OUNCES FRESH OR FROZEN PEAS
8 OUNCES TOMATO SAUCE
½ CUP WATER
2 TABLESPOONS CUMIN POWDER
1 LARGE YELLOW ONION
SALT AND PEPPER

A favorite recipe created by Arlene's mom. This ethnic dish is quick and easy but full of flavor!

Sauté onion in a small amount of olive oil. Add tomato sauce, water, cumin powder, salt and pepper to taste. Simmer for 15 minutes. Add peas and cook for an additional 5 minutes, just until al dente.

Variation: Add one cup cooked portuguese Linguisa sausage and you have a flavorful stew to serve with buttermilk mashed potatoes.

Serves 4.

POLENTA WITH ROASTED TOMATOES & THREE CHEESES

Slice tomatoes into wedges, mince garlic and chop onion. Combine vegetables and roast in a large roasting pan at 450 degrees for 2 to 3 hours, stirring often. Begin to add wine and broth as the liquid evaporates. Continue adding liquids 1/3 cup at a time. Roast until sauce is of desired consistency. Add sugar and salt and pepper to taste.

Bring water to a boil and whisk in polenta along with one teaspoon salt. Continue to whisk and simmer until polenta is slightly thickened. Add Parmesan cheese and pour into oiled 9x12 inch baking dish or oval gratin dish and cool.

Remove polenta to a cutting board and slice into 1-inch wide slices. Cover bottom of baking dish with 3/4 cup roasted tomato sauce. Arrange polenta and fontina cheese in alternating layers. Sprinkle with chopped basil. Spoon remaining roasted tomato sauce over polenta and top with crumbled Gorgonzola cheese. Bake uncovered for 45 minutes at 375 degrees. Let sit for five minutes then slice into squares and serve with your favorite salad.

Serves 6.

FOR ROASTED TOMATO SAUCE:
8 POUNDS TOMATOES, *very ripe*
16 GARLIC CLOVES
2 LARGE ONIONS
1 CUP DRY RED WINE
1 CUP VEGETABLE BROTH
2 TEASPOONS SUGAR
SALT & PEPPER

FOR THE POLENTA:
4 ½ CUPS WATER
1 ½ CUPS POLENTA
½ CUP PARMESAN CHEESE

TO ASSEMBLE:
8 OUNCES FONTINA CHEESE, *sliced*
6 OUNCES GORGONZOLA CHEESE, *crumbled*
½ CUP BASIL, *coarsely chopped*
1 ½ CUPS ROASTED TOMATO SAUCE

ROSEMARY CHICKEN WITH ROASTED GARLIC

Preheat oven to 425 degrees.

ONE 3-4 POUND CHICKEN
1 ½ CUPS CHICKEN STOCK
¾ CUP SHERRY WINE
3 LARGE SPRIGS ROSEMARY
ONE LARGE ONION
ONE HEAD GARLIC
8 SMALL NEW POTATOES
6 MEDIUM CARROTS
SALT AND PEPPER

A good "one pot" meal, easily prepared when time is short.

Place whole chicken in an oiled roasting pan. Insert rosemary and onion (halved) into cavity of chicken. Wedge potatoes and slice carrots. Break garlic head into cloves. Place carrots, potatoes and garlic around chicken. Pour chicken stock and sherry over the chicken. Season to taste with the salt and pepper. Roast at 425 degrees for 15 minutes. Lower oven temperature to 350 and roast for an additional 20 minutes or until juice runs clear when leg of chicken is pierced with fork.

Serves 3 to 4.

MRS. B's SPINACH SALAD

FOR THE DRESSING:

4 TEASPOONS SUGAR

1 TEASPOON DRY MUSTARD

⅓ CUP CIDER VINEGAR

1 CUP MILD OLIVE OIL

SALAD INGREDIENTS:

1 POUND BAG FRESH BABY SPINACH

1 HEAD RED LEAF LETTUCE
  torn into bite size pieces

½ POUND BACON, *cooked and drained*

3 HARD COOKED EGGS

1 SMALL RED ONION

4 OUNCES FETA CHEESE

Combine dressing ingredients and mix well.

Crumble bacon into small bits. Slice onion and chop eggs. Mix bacon, onion, eggs and cheese with greens, add dressing and toss salad. Season to taste with salt and pepper.

Serves 6-8.

THE GRINDLE ROOM RHYME

What should we do, where should we go?
We pondered these thoughts
While in Mendocino.

We ate and we slept,
We walked and ate more!
We sat and enjoyed the views of the shore.

Late night new friends
And cream sherry, too,
The parlor aglow with a warm firelight hue.

To Jim and Arlene, our gracious, kind hosts,
To others we meet,
Of you we will boast.

We've come but now gone,
Yet we'll come again
'Cause we love to retreat
To the J. Grindle Inn.

GIVE THE GIFT

<u>Mendocino Mornings</u> and a gift certificate for a stay at Joshua Grindle Inn. . . what a perfect gift for that someone who loves romance and good food!

Purchase by calling 1.800.GRINDLE. It's that simple. We will place the certificate inside the book and send it the next day.

Of course, the items can be purchased separately.

For other gift ideas from Joshua Grindle Inn, check out our website: www.joshgrin.com

INDEX

Recipes

INDEX

Ramblings